NOT YOUR YELLOW
FANTASY

NOT YOUR YELLOW FANTASY

DECONSTRUCTING THE LEGACY OF ASIAN FETISHIZATION

GIBOOM PARK

NEW DEGREE PRESS

COPYRIGHT © 2020 GIBOOM PARK

NOT YOUR YELLOW FANTASY

Deconstructing the Legacy of Asian Fetishization

ISBN   978-1-63676-582-2 *Paperback*
           978-1-63676-204-3 *Kindle Ebook*
           978-1-63676-205-0 *Ebook*

To the cold and lonely child.

CONTENTS

———

"One heart is not connected to another through harmony alone. They are, instead, linked deeply through their wounds. Pain linked to pain, fragility to fragility. There is no silence without a cry of grief, no forgiveness without bloodshed, no acceptance without a passage through acute loss. That is what lies at the root of true harmony."

—HARUKI MURAKAMI, COLORLESS TSUKURU
TAZAKI AND HIS YEARS OF PILGRIMAGE

CHAPTER 1

INTRODUCTION: THE BEST KIND

———

Standing in a corner at a fraternity party, I tried to adjust my eyes to the dimmed red lights sprinkled around the sweaty basement full of single-use plastic cups and first-year college students. Loud music blasted into my ears as blurry figures moved to the beat of the music. I glanced over at my phone, waiting for my friends to come back from their bathroom break, when a tall, broody white boy tapped me on my shoulder. He quickly leaned in, loudly exclaiming into my ear:

"Hey! Are you Asian?"

Clearly ignoring how uncomfortable I felt in his close proximity, he stood still, waiting for my response.

"Uh... yes..?" I responded, baffled by his question.

My jet-black hair, slanted deep brown eyes, and round facial structure were all pretty indicative of my Korean heritage. It wasn't as if it was a mystery that I was Asian.

"What kind?" he quickly responded.

I felt my heart *drop.*

What kind? What kind of question was that? Was he talking about what drink I wanted?

I stared at him, waiting for him to maybe slip up a smile or laugh to help me understand he was joking. He stared into my eyes, persisting in all seriousness.

"Uh... I'm not too sure if this is what you were asking? But... uh... I'm Korean... American," I answered, clinging on to the 2 percent of desperate hope I had inside of me thinking I simply misunderstood his question.

"Oh, that's the best kind."

***

Despite the obvious disgust and horror I displayed toward him almost immediately, the same boy tried to follow me around the party for the rest of the night, continuing to bombard me with questions of whether or not I had "been to Seoul" or if I "spoke any Asian languages." My arms began to tense up as an inexplicable pressure built up in my chest, and my mind scrambled to come up with a response, trying to portray the odd mixture of sadness, hurt, and rage I was feeling within my frazzled head.

At one point of the night, one of the friends I had gone to the party with yelled in annoyance at the boy, "You know I'm half-Korean too, right?" Although he had ignored her for most of the night, his eyes suddenly lit up and shifted to my friend, now suddenly "curious" of her identity.

It was horrifying how quickly someone's words could make me feel so *worthless*. The second the words *"the best kind"* slithered out of his lips, my mouth failed to formulate a response. My heart was pounding against my chest, begging me to *say something—to say anything*. And yet, as if time and space had stood still in the five inches between this boy and me , I could only silently sigh in my internal dialogue.

Later that night, I overheard him tell his friend he was going to take me home—I panicked, fidgeting my way toward my friends so they could get me out of the party. As he continued to ignore my rejection of his advances, my friends grabbed my hands and dashed out the back door of the house. As we were running away from the fraternity, I saw his face in the corner of my eye, chasing us while yelling, "Wait, hey! I told you to stop. Wait!"

Unfortunately, this wasn't the first time I would encounter yellow fever, nor would it be the last.

***

GRAPPLING WITH TRUTH

Like most East and Southeast Asians of the diaspora, I learned what *yellow fever*, or the derogatory term used to define an Asian fetish, was at a young age. *Yellow fever*, or Asian fetishization, is known as the **sexual or romantic preference for Asian individuals with an emphasis on East and Southeast Asian women and other gender minorities perceived as women.**

Despite the lack of resources available to read up on the topic or overall conversation in society on this "taboo" topic, I was quite familiar with it from lived experience. From the internet comments I received as a kid on social media about how beautiful my "pale skin and black hair was," to the catcalls asking about my "slanted pussy" I received as a fifteen-year-old rushing the streets of New York to get to my sister's graduation on time, by the time I was an adult I was already accustomed to hearing sexual comments about my ethnicity.

It became something so normalized, something my friends and I would always joke about in school whenever one of our Asian female peers would date a non-Asian male or when we would get hit on by someone who would compliment our looks. We would jokingly label someone in our class as "the guy with the severe case of *yellow fever*" for constantly only dating Asians, then laugh off the reality that it was simply "odd," to say the least. As I entered the world of online dating, this became even more prevalent—guys would message me that they had a sexual thing for Asian girls and ask if my

"Asian vagina" was "smaller-than-average." They would ask if they could eat me like "fried rice" and if I wanted to suck the dicks of my "oppressors."

The reality that fetishization was a prominent phenomenon looming over the East and Southeast Asian American community was something we all seemed to be aware of— something we had all become normalized to, despite never understanding why or how this *yellow fever* had infiltrated our world.

I was no different.

I was accustomed to using comedy as a way to collectively laugh at the sexual racism that was, frankly speaking, quite bothersome. A part of me had simply accepted I was going to hear these comments in the dating world, and some men were going to only be attracted to me because of my Asian ethnicity. To be frank, at a certain point, I started to even try taking it as a compliment; I was so used to guys telling me to *learn how to take a compliment* when I expressed disgust toward being considered an "exotic" race.

I simply felt as if it was *my fault* for being treated that way. If I couldn't escape this disgust, the only way to take minimal control in this situation was to bury my emotions and accept it as flattery.

That night, however, as the words "the best kind of Asian" came out of the mouth of a fellow student at what was supposedly one of the most intellectual institutions in the entire world, I couldn't help but feel this overwhelming frustration and confusion of the inability to escape this bigotry and racist objectification. I had convinced myself that once I entered college, the remnants of ignorant fetishizing would magically disappear. *It had to.* I had been maintaining this broken identity through a fine string of hope that certain spaces of intellectual minds could protect me from my history of experiencing such disgust.

Unfortunately that night, I came to terms with my own blatant ignorance. I was wrong.

Artwork by *Azelia Lau*

Staring into the gray ceiling of my dingy bland dorm that hummed a small tune in rhythm to the air conditioner, I sighed in frustration at the lack of awareness I had about what exactly this *yellow fever* was and how it had become such a disgusting, but fairly normal, aspect of my life.

Why was it that, despite the lack of representation Asian individuals generally received from Western media, Asian women were so sexualized? Why was it that often Asian men were rejected or generalized to be effeminate beings? Was it really okay for people to have a "racial preference" when it came to their sexual attraction? If so, why did it make me feel so *worthless* every time my yellow skin color was explicitly the one trait that made me attractive to someone?

Why had a part of me simply accepted it as a facet of my reality, falsely convincing myself that this had more benefits than consequences to my life as I was fortunate to be a part of a race that was "preferred?" Why were Asian women presumed to be stereotyped as a monolithic group, oftentimes emphasizing only the East Asian countries and their influences?

Why was it, as an Asian American woman, I had none of the answers to these questions?

To answer these questions, I decided to start a research project of my own—a project simply meant to educate *myself*—and to become more aware of the microaggressions I had witnessed and buried as a kid.

I decided to extensively study yellow fever.

AN INTROSPECTIVE VOYAGE

Thus started a year-long project of sifting through articles, research studies, and textbooks. I collected qualitative interviews from not only professors, authors, and influencers, but also from normal everyday individuals who had witnessed or experienced this *yellow fever*, aiming to learn from their experiences.

I infiltrated spaces I never imagined myself going into, like incel groups and misogynistic communities, to better understand individuals with completely different ideologies and views from mine, and to see how they treated the subject of sexual racism. Investigating the plethora of questions embedded in the backburner of my mind regarding my ignorance of the depths of *yellow fever*, it was evident these were questions that had answers not a lot of individuals were aware of in the first place.

Terms like *yellow fever, jungle fever, salsa fever, curry fever,* and other derogatory phrases like these are common in daily rhetoric and slang. Its implications and historical roots were often unknown to their users. Similarly to how I had simply accepted Asian fetishization and the prominence of *yellow fever,* which I frequently perpetuated myself, many of those around me were equally clueless to how everything had "started" and how it so easily became embedded into our identities.

Additionally, my personal project on *yellow fever* revealed a much darker and insidious reality than the one I thought I had always known. Like many others, I was only aware of *yellow fever* and the prevalence of Asian fetishization in common everyday subject matters like dating apps and inter-racial relationships.

However, I quickly found Asian fetishization to be related to other topics outside of everyday dating apps and everyday catcalling, oftentimes much more insidious such as:

- Sexual Imperialism and Military Intervention

- "Yellow Peril" and Xenophobia

- Human Trafficking, Mail-Order Brides, and Sex Tourism

- Alt-Rights, Incels, and White Supremacists

- Pornography and Child Exploitation

- Rejection and Emasculation of Asian men

- Disease and Pandemics

Despite Asian fetishization often being seen as a very "black and white" subject matter with two-dimensionality in its overtone, it was in reality often interrelated to other harmful Asian stereotypes such as the Model Minority Myth, the Perpetual Foreigner stereotype, as well as with elements of the "White Man's Burden." It tied into elements of white supremacy and anti-BIPOC (Black, Indigenous, and People of Color) sentiment, as well as how these relations were related to implications such as gender-based violence and harmful monolithic assumptions. It was connected to how Asian bodies were often considered "diseased" or subpar to white bodies. This narrative promotes the idea that BIPOC bodies are simply not enough.

Everything seemed to intersect in deep tragedy, rousing in its horrific "glory."

***

CRIPPLING APATHY

Unfortunately, conversations about the topic of *yellow fever* and racial fetishization are often a conversation many individuals do not care about or want to have. Many viewed my curiosity as a waste of time and another obstacle they felt they needed to overcome. I was constantly used to hearing "attraction is attraction" and "what's wrong with having a preference for Asians or for any race in general?"

People defensively argued that racial preference is out of one's control, strongly persisting in the idea that having a preference is harmless. With the small check of a box in a dating app, algorithms could help "filter" out races for many individuals, "harmlessly" ranking certain ethnicities over others based on one's "preference." With the click of a button, one could have unlimited access to ethnically focused pornography, feeding into the attraction they had for a certain race.

"No one is getting hurt, so why should I care?"

These racial-based preferences had all become so normalized. It was uncomfortable to even question them.

Although discouraged by such negativity and unwillingness, I began to realize these reactions were precisely the reason I needed to share my story with everyone. To instigate change, I had to initiate uncomfortable conversations. The "taboo" and uncomfortable discussions needed to occur.

A TALE OF TRUTH

My book is intended to tell you precisely why you should care and why it is not, in fact, "harmless." My book will prove there is no such thing as a "harmless" racial preference, and it will show you how sexual racism is a living, breathing creature amidst our society today. This book will shine a light on the urgency of the topic and how the tips of Asian fetishization feed into the exploitation and commodification of Asian women and children.

That said, this book is not merely a combination of facts and historical events, but a painful recalling of not only my experience with Asian fetishization, but of my community's. Gaslighted, overlooked, and ignored, this is for all my fellow Asian women of the diaspora who are unable to speak out about their own pain.

A story of our experiences—our pain—
overlooked for far too long.

This book is for anyone open to educating themselves about Asian fetishization, and how it plays into multifaceted crimes and hurtful actions. It is for anyone who struggled or continues to struggle to comprehend the roots of this racial bias and the oppressive aspects of sexual racism regarding Asian fetishization. It is also for anyone who wants to be an ally for BIPOC individuals, fighting against the systemic racism that oppresses marginalized communities in one way or another, and in this case—sexual racism. My book is not an academic study nor a history book (nor should it be taken as one), but a combination of personal narrative and impactful research that will hopefully change your mind in how you view, and more importantly, *feel* about *yellow fever*.

With that in mind, I do want to make it clear my book mostly pertains to heterosexual East and Southeast Asian American and Asian women. In no way am I trying to deconstruct the validity and struggles of the LGBTQ+ community, nor other racial minorities who are also affected by sexual racism by using the term *yellow fever* throughout my book. My intention is to simply exemplify the unfortunate reality of how *yellow fever* tends to place a heavy emphasis on a certain type of individual from a very specific region in the world in its harmful stereotyping manner.

The start of any journey begins with a question, and for me, that question was *what is yellow fever*?

As you'll see in the next chapter, it's not so easy to define, and the journey to how we got to where we are is winding and dark. The journey to self-discovery is never clear. You light the way to your own questions on unconscious bias and prejudice.

No matter how many times I was repeatedly traumatized by the racist, degrading words I would hear from men throughout my life, I couldn't help but feel as if it was my responsibility to bear with it. If anything, I was the one being too sensitive. Overly dramatic.

To this day, I ask myself: Why did I hurt myself for being hurt?

—ANONYMOUS ASIAN AMERICAN
WOMAN IN HER LATE TWENTIES

CHAPTER 2

WHAT IS YELLOW FEVER?

Casually walking through the cafeteria of my suburban middle school, quiet whispers flooded my surroundings as I turned around to see my Asian American friend, Julie, walking across the cafeteria holding hands with her new boyfriend, a curly-haired white boy named George.

I sat down at a table with my friends when the girl sitting next to me quietly muttered in my ear, "Why is she dating someone with *yellow fever*? I don't understand." I carefully looked at George from the corner of my eye, watching him heartily laugh in conversation with Julie.

"What's *yellow fever*?" I cluelessly asked my friend as I munched down on my very mediocre burger.

"You're so naive," she responded. "There's no way you don't know."

I quickly realized the soundtrack of whispering occurring in the cafeteria was from my Asian American peers staring at this newfound couple. I looked back at my friend in confusion, unable to piece together why so many individuals seemed utterly disgusted by them, and to be more exact, disgusted with *him*.

Frankly speaking, I was generally disinterested in school affairs and was confused as to why so many individuals were invested in them as a couple.

She sighed in disappointment at my cluelessness, finally accepting I was unaware of what she meant by *yellow fever*. She rolled her eyes, pushed her lunch to the side, and blatantly stared at me.

"Listen. George only dates Asian girls. Julie just happens to fit the pattern."

"What do you mean he only dates Asian girls?" I asked cautiously.

"It's exactly what it sounds like. If you're Asian, you're attractive to him. Nothing more, nothing less."

***

I spent the next few days trying to understand what it meant to be attractive *because* of your race.

It was an odd conversation to have, one I don't think my eleven-year-old brain was able to fully comprehend at the moment. It made me uneasy to think that one's particular race could be the sole reason a person could be attracted to another person. It seemed as if the clamor of attention from my peers ended the second we exited the school building. As if there was an artificial on and off switch of disgust, George's dating patterns only seemed to be treated like a problematic topic within our cafeteria's walls. No one was conversing about it, pointing it out, or talking about it in any form of a solemn tone, so how could I?

This was how *yellow fever* left an imprint on me at the age of eleven, slowly but surely mutating a long-term belief that Asian fetishization was indeed "normal." In the next few weeks, no, *years* of school, I witnessed George's consistent "preference" in his dating standards. He dated Julie for a time, and, as many middle school relationships do, they broke up. I then saw him date Kim, Tiffany, and Jessica, watching him rotate between some of them at times, returning to a different Asian girl in between. By the time I graduated from high school, I lost track of exactly how many Asian girls he had dated.

For over a decade, the questions I had for George remained frozen in the subconscious of my hurt. What exactly was *yellow fever,* and how was liking someone for their race a societally acceptable phenomenon? Why did it make me feel so uncomfortable, yet so silent and helpless? Why did I feel the need to hide my hurt for the sake of the status quo?

To answer these questions, I needed to start from square one: defining *yellow fever*.

SEARCHING FOR A DEFINITION

To define *yellow fever*, I sought out related documents and research materials that could potentially point me in the right direction. Soon, however, I realized there was an extreme lack of **material** on *yellow fever*.

Despite its colloquial commonality and relevance in the Asian American community, it was surprisingly a complicated subject matter to research due to the lack of sources extensively and empirically studying it. Simply searching the terms "Asian woman" and "Asian female" on Google brought up an abundance of photographs and articles that made it seem as if these individuals were commodities on sale. In comparison, Asian fetishization and *yellow fever* lacked in official definitions and substantial research to maintain its validity.

Instead, I found an abundance of *yellow fever* referenced in crowdsourced dictionaries, comic skits, and in popular media. For example, I was able to find more than six "official" definitions listed in the Urban Dictionary for *yellow fever*, a contemporary online dictionary where users define vernacular slang.[1] There were frequent mentions *of yellow fever* in blogs, newspapers, and online articles, often conversed about in smaller online communities. I found it loosely referenced in media, such as comedian Amy Schumer's stand-up routine

_____

1   *Urban Dictionary*, s.v. "Yellow Fever," accessed February 12, 2020.

"Mostly Sexy Stuff," where she lists how she can't "compete with an Asian chick" because they have "naturally silky hair" and "the smallest vaginas in the game."[2] From the horrific song "Asian Girlz" by the band Day Above Ground in 2013 to the culturally appropriating and highly sexualized "Chun-Li" character in Capcom's Street Fighter, it wasn't hard to find elements of Asian fetishization in popular media.[3],[4]

In these references, Asian women always seemed to be depicted through a dichotomous stereotype generalizing them as "manipulative and untrustworthy" or "faceless, quiet and invisible... sexual objects."[5] Other stereotypes perpetuated the idea that Asian women had "different sexual organs," such as small vaginas, "slanted" or "sideways" vaginas as well as other sexual deformities.

For example, according to Historian Judy Yung and her book *Unbound Voices: A Documentary History of Chinese Women in San Francisco*, the "ongoing myth that the vaginal opening of a Chinese woman was horizontal rather than vertical has been circulating as folklore since the 1850s," as Asian women

---

2   Amy Schumer, *Amy Schumer: Mostly Sex Stuff*, August 18, 2012, TV comedy special, video.

3   "Asian Girlz Lyrics: Day Above Ground," Genius, accessed February 12, 2020.

4   "Street Fighter Champion Edition: Chun-Li." Capcom, accessed February 14, 2020.

5   S. Mukkamala and K. L. Suyemoto, "Racialized Sexism/Sexualized Racism: A Multimethod Study of Intersectional Experiences of Discrimination for Asian American Women," *Asian American Journal of Psychology* 9, no. 1 (2018): 32–46.

found themselves sold into sex trafficking and slavery during the California Gold Rush.[6] Western history seemed to have consistently portrayed Asian women of the diaspora in a sexually illuminating light, bleeding into their perception in modern-day society.

These sources helped me put together that the definition of *yellow fever* was the **derogatory term used to define an Asian fetish, otherwise known as the sexual or romantic preference for Asian individuals, especially East Asian and Southeast Asian women (and other gender minorities perceived as women).** It often pertained to the barbaric and primitive underlying sexual stereotypes projected upon Asian women when fetishized, dehumanizing them to nothing more than a fantasy.

Yellow fever was simply an overall umbrella term used to negatively describe the commodification of Asian individuals, especially women, and their hypersexualization in society, especially in societies that are dominantly white like the United States.

ATTRACTION VERSUS FETISH

With the definition of *yellow fever* in mind, I wanted to then look into why a racial fetish was different from other sexual fetishes. A large part of my discomfort in expressing my own qualms against Asian fetishization derived from individuals

---

6   Judy Yung, "Bound Feet: Nineteenth Century." Chapter. In *Unbound Voices: A Documentary History of Chinese Women in San Francisco.* Berkeley, CA: University of California Press, 1999.

and communities who constantly told me that an Asian fetish was no different from something like "having a thing for brunettes" or "having a thing for feet." They claimed the Asian fetish, as well as other racial fetishes, was simply a preference for specific phenotypes that *happened to* pertain to Asian individuals.

"We can't control whom we're attracted to. We just have a thing for Asians. What's so wrong about that?"

I was accustomed to individuals arguing they could not control whom they were attracted to, and, to them, a specific race could simply be more attractive than the others. It was all a harmless, biological preference in their eyes. It was something I personally struggled with understanding as well, as I initially agreed to their persuasive argument that seemingly held ethical weight.

Research studies and surveys conducted have also shown individuals to argue for this "preference" for phenotypical traits argument. For example, in a research study by Bitna Kim in 2011, one of the men questioned why an Asian fetish was different from other forms of attractions and why it had a negative "fetish" label, when attractions to other phenotypes, like blondes, were not described as a "blonde fetish."[7]

---

7   Bitna Kim, "Asian Female and Caucasian Male Couples: Exploring the Attraction." *Pastoral Psychology* 60, no. 2 (2010): 233–44.

So what made an Asian fetish different from a "blonde fetish?" Was it really acceptable?

An Asian fetish, like other racial fetishes, is different from other types of fetishes and kinks because they are not about the sexualization of a body part, a self-chosen lifestyle, nor a specific choice of action. Racial fetishes (such as the derogatory terms of *yellow, jungle, curry,* and *salsa fever*) are about the stereotyping and exotification of large groups of people based on their racial identities.[8]

Whereas people can have a preference for a certain sexual lifestyle, action, or body part, race is not equivalent to these preferences in that it cannot be prejudiced to hold certain characteristics fulfilling one's projections. In other words, it is absolutely absurd to treat something like a "foot fetish" as the same thing as a racial fetish because race includes much more than the phenotypic, physical attributes—it also includes the historical and cultural elements of an individual's being.

This ties into the idea of "sexual racism," or the term coined in the 1970s by Rutgers Professor Stember as "the sexual rejection of the racial minority" and the "conscious attempt on the part of the majority to prevent interracial cohabitation."[9]

---

8   Chin Lu, "Why Yellow Fever Is Different Than 'Having a Type'," *The Bold Italic Editors,* June 3, 2013.

9   Norman Lederer, "Charles Herbert Stember. Sexual Racism: The Emotional Barrier to an Integrated Society. Pp. Xviii, 234. New York: Elsevier,

Through people justifying their racial prejudice under the disguise of "preference," it perpetuates sexual racism within our society as it ranks groups of people above and under others.

Human beings are simply reduced to the characteristics that they are stereotyped to their race, becoming objectified based on their phenotypes to exist accordingly to the fulfillment of the seeker.

1976. $13.50 - Norman Lederer, 1978." SAGE Journals, September 1, 1978.

Photograph by Jingyuan Tian

Instead of emphasizing the individual's character, humanity, and overall person, it was this fantasy one had of a race that was a priority above all. This fantasy was the very same reason why certain races were "preferred," and why some races were rejected, inherently ranking them on a spectrum of attractiveness and sexualization. "'Racial preferences,'" as writer Aaron Mok puts it, "aren't static, objective truths that you are born with." Instead, "they are an amalgamation of systematic injustices, one's unique circumstances and one's ignorance."[10]

I noticed a similar sentiment in an interview I had with Ryu, a twenty-year-old college student I reached out to regarding the topic. She shared that she had met a white boy at a college party who talked a lot about a three-month study abroad program he did in China. She initially thought he was "cool" until she saw his room for the first time. He had two panda plushies, Chinese good luck signs plastered around his walls, and a few other China-related decorations. She also saw that he loved green tea and was very proud of his distinctly Chinese tea collection. She later caught him admitting to her that to him, all Asian girls were a default "7." In other words, this boy's fascination and obsession with Asian culture, and specifically Chinese culture, extended toward human beings themselves, objectifying them and unifying them with his fantasy of China.

The dehumanization that occurs with racial fetishization is visible by the overall undermining of the personal experiences of individuals experiencing racial fetishization themselves by defenders of their "racial preference." By defending one's attraction to an entire ethnicity, one is thus objectifying

---

10   Kelsey Yandura, "Racial Dating Preferences: Racist Excuses or Inherent Desires?" *Rewire*, February 25, 2020.

the individual and ignoring the personal experiences, the trauma, and the microaggressions that accompany these racial fetishes. For example, in multiple interviews I had with Asian American individuals, most of them commented they had to be cautious, in fear of being attractive to someone solely because of their ethnicity and not their character. Several also mentioned that when they attempted to question if their partners were dating them because of their ethnicity, some would violently lash back in defense, questioning why it was so wrong to be attracted to someone because of their race.

I conducted another personal interview with Lee, a twenty-two-year-old recent college graduate. She found it disheartening when dating a guy with so-called *yellow fever*, that he, as a non-Asian man, was able to experience and "take all of the best, fun parts of being Korean or Asian (K-POP, food), but not experience the stereotypes, the racism, and the xenophobia" she witnessed as an Asian American woman. No matter how much she wanted them to understand and how much these comments made her feel so small, to these guys, **their "preference" was a priority over her hurt and pain.**

JUST A "PREFERENCE"

In addition, the argument that it is simply a phenotypic attraction like a "blonde fetish" that happens to be race-related fails because, unlike being "blonde," race cannot be limited and derived to only be "phenotypic." Looking to Robin Zheng, an assistant professor of philosophy at Yale-NUS in Singapore, and her summary of this defense in which she summarizes as the Mere Preferences Argument (MPA), defenders of racial fetishes claim that:

1. There is "nothing morally objectionable about sexual preferences for... non-racialized phenotypic traits."

2. "Preferences for racialized physical traits are no different from preferences for non-racialized phenotypic traits."

3. Thus, these "preferences" are "not morally objectionable."[11]

Zheng points out that the MPA's main argument lies around the assumption of "minimal race."[12] Minimal race, Zheng writes, "is a classification scheme whereby humans are divided into clusters of phenotypic traits along with geographical ancestry but without ascriptions of any particular physical, mental, or moral traits to these different groups."[13]

In other words, MPA's argument on preference only holds true in a "post-racial" society where race holds no significance. However, it is impossible to separate Asian American and Asian individuals, as well as any BIPOC individual, from the cultural and societal traits that subconsciously and consciously ascribe to the phenotypic traits of the individual. Our society is not a "post-racial" society, as seen by countless cases of police brutality against Black individuals, the treatment of Asian Americans during the COVID-19 outbreak, and the continuance of detention centers that maintain horrific living conditions. We are still a highly racially

---

11 Robin Zheng, "Why Yellow Fever Isn't Flattering: A Case Against Racial Fetishes." *Journal of the American Philosophical Association* 2, no. 3 (2016): 400–419.

12 Ibid.

13 Ibid.

divided society that naturally allows for certain connotations to derive from one's race. Similarly to individuals that like to argue they "don't see race" or don't understand why "BIPOC make everything about race," the MPA argument tends to dismiss the reality of our current society.

Furthermore, as being of Asian descent represents more than forty-eight different nationalities with different phenotypic traits, it is absurd even to argue that one is "attracted to an Asian's physical traits."[14] This promotes the false sentiment that all Asian individuals have similar characteristics and phenotypes, once again returning to the comfort and fantasy of the perpetuator of this *yellow fever* more than the reality of individuals of Asian descent. Through accepting racial "preference," we would be allowing for the complete ignorance of the pain impacted upon individuals suffering from this racial fetishization for the sake of the status quo's comfort and ease. It also promotes this false monolithic sexualization of Asians, which fails to acknowledge the existence of darker-skinned Asians.

The racial "preference" argument is a tool used by perpetrators to maintain their comfort and ease, preserving their fantasy of what a "race" represents, projecting one's own expectations upon an entire racial group. Specifically, in regard to Asian individuals, it diminishes the pain of individuals who have been fetishized and rejected, the urgency in the need to disaggregate what "Asian" represents through

---

14   "Census Data & API Identities," Asian Pacific Institute on Gender-Based Violence, accessed March 8, 2020.

its monolithic assumptions, while providing the ability to objectify individuals for their phenotypic traits.

ILLUMINATING CURIOSITY

In summary, I was able to find that *yellow fever* was an extremely problematic yet overlooked phenomenon. It not only projected a fantasy of Asian women, but also somehow managed to mask itself under the problematic justification of racial "preference," a justification the general public seemed to agree with. It promoted the monolithic stereotyping of all Asian individuals, dehumanizing and commodifying the phenotypes of East and Southeast Asians and displaying it as a representation for all Asians.

I was now better aware of the definition of *yellow fever* outside of the premature understanding I developed as an eleven-year-old. It had become much clearer to me why I felt uncomfortable watching George date based on race, and to see why it was clearly problematic for individuals to defend racial fetishes. Normalization was perhaps the option I had used to escape from my own ignorance and cluelessness. However, it did not erase the reality of how harmful fetishization was not only to myself, but to society in general.

There were still a few questions begging for answers in the illumination and extension of my preexisting knowledge. Where exactly did *yellow fever* come from, and how did it become so widespread? Why were there stereotypes interlaced with the concept of *yellow fever?* What effects did such dichotomous stereotypes have in society?

As you will find in the next chapter, the next steps of my journey were to embark on a historical analysis to seek answers to these burning questions. To fully understand the subject, it is necessary to comprehend and to potentially empathize with how fetishization is related to topics of Western literature, white imperialism, and Hollywood media.

The second I entered his bedroom, I saw hentai posters all across his walls and random Japanese anime figures decorating the corners of his desk. There was also this blue silk kimono draped across his chair. As I caught a glimpse of my reflection in his mirror, I couldn't help but wonder...

Was I simply another addition to his "collection"?

— ANONYMOUS CHINESE AMERICAN
INTERVIEWEE IN HER TWENTIES

CHAPTER 3

ECHOES OF HISTORY

"*Danyeo-oget-seumnida!*" (I'll be back!) I cheeringly yelled across our apartment, hoping that my words would reach past the overlapping sounds of the angry Korean anchors debating loudly on my mother's daily dose of morning KBS news. I caught a short glimpse of my mom smiling at me before I threw on my knock-off Adidas sneakers, quickly brushing through my tangled hair in front of the hallway mirror. I promptly gave my dad a hurried bear hug, tensely running out the door in an attempt to catch the ever-early school bus.

As a kid, it was my everyday routine to *show* my parents that I was "happy." It was like playing the lead in a one-man show—except my role was a never-ending masquerade full of changing partners and ballgowns, all hiding the stinky, rotting flesh behind the facade of exquisite "happiness." The second these curtains faded, the spotlight illuminating me shined its face away, leaving me to grapple with a solemn shadow gripping my sanity in unbearable anxiety.

The shadow otherwise known as school.

***

"Ni Hao" or "Konnichiwa?"

*"Giboom? What kind of name is that? It sounds like
Baboon."*

*"So I have a genuine question—is it harder to see
because your eyes are so small?"*

"Ew, what is that? Is that dog? You eat dog?"

School to me felt like an *animal kingdom*—full of savage-like
lions and haunting hyenas waiting to pounce upon me at
every turn. Each morning I would dread stepping onto the
hard cement floors of my school entrance, afraid of the words
I would hear this time and the potential ways I would come
to *hate myself,* or rather my skin color.

As a Korean American from a low-income family, it wasn't
difficult to stand out in a predominantly white school in an
upper-class neighborhood. While my blonde-haired peers
were carrying their Vera Bradley lunchboxes and wearing
their brand-new Abercrombie & Fitch outfits, my jet-black
hair and secondhand clothes stuck out like a sore thumb.
Perhaps this distinction between *them* and me was why my
school life seemed riddled with microaggressions and endless
hints of racism that pricked off ends of my self-esteem.

Walking down the narrow hallways of my school building,
guys would often run up to me to bow with their hands in
a prayer pose, iterating "Konnichiwa" and "Ni Hao" to me,

fully aware I was perfectly fluent in English. They would then pull their eyes back to imitate my "chinky eyes," finishing off the interaction with high-pitched Kung-Fu fighting noises. The cafeteria was a haunting jungle where the do-shi-rak (lunchbox) my mother would so carefully pack every morning would become an item of repulsion and disgust to many. *"What are you eating...?"* they would gapingly ask, my "smelly" kimchi becoming a source of high fascination. Soon enough, bathroom stalls became my very best friends—a safe haven far away from eyes and their brown bags full of PB&J sandwiches.

"Oh her? The Asian girl who's good at math and quiet?" became the way I was known. I was the "girl with the slanted eyes" who was "probably from China," whatever that was supposed to mean. I was always the "foreigner" no matter how many times I told them my favorite singer was Justin Bieber or that I watched the latest episode of Pretty Little Liars. Every day meant a new way my peers could emphasize how *different* I was.

All I ever wanted was to be accepted, but to them, it seemed that my ethnicity was enough of a reason for me not to be enough.

A VULGAR DISCONNECT
Years passed, and I eventually become accustomed to being the "shy" and "quiet" Asian girl after years of labeling and perpetual stereotyping. It was thus so odd when I began to realize that, as I was getting older, these microaggressions

and racist tendencies from those around me were shifting into something so... vulgar?

Despite remaining unchanged from the introverted Asian American girl trying to eat her "smelly" do-si-rak in the bathroom—away from all of her white peers making fun of her—and remaining the very same girl who would pull her eyes wide at night to run away from the haunting whispers of "chinky," the world began to paint me in a different light—a light blatantly... sexual.

Microaggressions like "Konnichiwa" and "Ni hao" for the remainder of my elementary school days transformed into up-and-down looks combined with "I've never been with an Asian before." Comments about my kimchi and my "skills in math" became inquiries about my body, as men would mindlessly iterate to me: "I bet your vagina is tight and slanted, just like your eyes." Some would mindlessly declare, "I want to dominate your small body, chink" to "can you cure my *yellow fever*? I'll aggressively fuck you." Others asked if I had been with "a real man with a big non-Asian dick" to satisfy my "Oriental pussy."

"I want to dominate your small body, chink"

"Can you cure my yellow fever?"

*"I bet your vagina is tight and slanted, just like
your eyes"*

I was, at most, perhaps fifteen, when I had begun to personally hear these phrases. A student stuck in her formative teenage years, barely even knowledgeable of her own sexuality. It was as if I was thrown into a cold river of sexual illumination, unaware of how to swim against this stream of newfound cruelty.

I wasn't aware of how to navigate such cold brutality. I felt too inadequate—no, too ashamed—to share such pain with my own parents. Like many children of immigrant families, I felt it was my duty to protect my parents from the harms of racism, from the words that left haunting scratches on my soul. I wanted to convince them I was truly their *American Dream*—that their sacrifices, full of blood, sweat, and tears, were effectively maximized through the remnants of my future. I refused to translate racist comments they would hear from strangers. I pretended the man on the AT&T callline wasn't yelling at them to "speak better English." I wanted to hide my parents from the emotional drought that parched my soul, in an attempt to at least "save" them from the cruelty I experienced. So how could I possibly mention such demoralizing fetishization I was suddenly encountering?

I was utterly confused. How had I suddenly gone from being seen as the "foreign nerdy girl" to suddenly being the "exotic" and "Oriental" Asian girl? Was I supposed to be delighted I was finally getting some form of attention, despite still feeling rotten inside? Was this a compliment that I was attractive now? Or simply another perpetuation of how I was being seen as "different" again? Sure, my body was changing into that of a mature, older woman, but the small child within me was still shaking, afraid of this inexplainable difference in how I was perceived.

What was this disconnect in my identity—or rather, **their depiction of my identity?**

UNBURYING THE TRAUMA

For the next process of my research, I revisited these sentiments I left unanswered in my internal void. Where had these sexual stereotypes of Asian women being either docile sexual dolls or mysterious and "exotic" women come from? East and Southeast Asian women were always seen as binary representations of either the "Dragon Lady" or the "Lotus Blossom," "geisha," and "China Doll." The "Dragon Lady" was the conception that Asian females were treacherous and seductive beings who could use their aggressiveness and sexuality to manipulate men. The "Lotus Blossom," "geisha," and "China Doll," stereotype was the idea that Asian women were *objects* based on Western male sexual fantasy, a product of colonial and military powers, but why?

Where had these comments these men imbued on my identity come from, and why were their tones so power-driven, aggressive, and demandingly haughty? Asian fetishization sexualized Asian women, dehumanizing them to nothing but their sexual features projected upon a fantasy—but why? And more importantly, how?

MADAME BUTTERFLY

Historians postulate the sexualization and Western subjugation of Asian women that feed Asian fetishization is said to reach all the way back to Marco Polo's travels on the Silk

Road.[15] The portrayal of the Asian and Asian American woman as exotic "Lotus Blossoms," one of the two dichotomic sexual stereotypes projected upon Asian women, however, can be found in Western literature and media, tracing back to the 1800s.

Artwork by Yu-Chieh Wang

---

15   Yuan Ren, "'Yellow Fever' Fetish: Why Do So Many White Men Want to Date a Chinese woman?" *The Telegraph*, July 1, 2014.

In 1887, French novelist Pierre Loti wrote *Madame Chrysan-thème,* a semi-autobiographic story of a naval officer who took on a Japanese woman in Nagasaki as a temporary wife.[16] In the novel, the author described his temporary wife, Kiku (Chrysanthemum) née Kane, to be a delicate plaything he encountered and took a hold of in the "Orient." He treasured his "little, creamy-skinned woman with black hair and cat's eyes," whom he compared to being not "much bigger than a doll."[17] The naval officer, who eventually left his temporary "doll" behind to return to his "normal" life in Europe, could control and sexually play with the "submissive" Japanese woman and could quickly abandon her if necessary. His authority in this situation emphasized the idea that "Oriental" women were submissive beings for entertainment objectified for the benefit of white men.[18]

This novel heavily influenced how the Western world saw Japan, as at the time international travel was rare. In contrast, international trade, including the trade of literature and art, were more common. The novel and the perspective of Asian women it took consequently affected how the Western world viewed Asian women and their roles in society, as the novel served as a perspective-giver of the "Orient." Japanese women were simply playthings to Loti, and subsequently, the individuals he called "china ornaments" became playthings to the Western hemisphere as well.[19] They were easily abandoned

---

16   Pierre Loti, Madame Chrysanthème. 1887.

17   Ibid.

18   Ibid.

19   Ibid.

individuals who needed a white male to "save them" and who were submissive sexual objects, obedient to their male figures.

This storyline of the white, European male leaving his submissive, "Oriental" sex object became a popularized plot that continued its legacy in different forms. In *Madame Butterfly*, an opera in 1904 by Giacomo Puccini, Cio-Cio San (Butterfly), a fifteen-year old Japanese maiden falls in love with an American navy lieutenant named Pinkerton.[20] Although Cio-Cio San herself is excited to marry an American because she recently converted to Christianity, Pinkerton marries her out of convenience with plans to leave her in the near future. After spending their first night together, the lieutenant quickly leaves for the United States. Three years pass and Cio-Cio San waits for Pinkerton's return. She alerts the American consul, Sharpless, that she has given birth to Pinkerton's son while he was away. Pinkerton finally returns to Japan to see Cio-Cio San, bringing along his American wife, Kate. Pinkerton realizes he has made a mistake when he arrives, noticing Cio-Cio San's efforts in decorating the house for his return; he quickly hides away from Cio-Cio San, admitting his cowardice and mistake. Cio-Cio San, agrees to give her son to Kate and Pinkerton only if Pinkerton comes to see her for himself. The opera ends with Cio-Cio San praying to her ancestral gods, saying farewell to her son, placing an American flag in her son's hands, and committing suicide with her father's seppuku knife.[21]

---

20 Giacomo Puccini, "Madam Butterfly." February 17, 1904.

21 Ibid.

Artwork by Yu-Chieh Wang

Similarly to *Madame Chrysanthème, Madame Butterfly* portrays the Asian girl as an "Oriental" doll, allowing Pinkerton to abandon the fifteen-year-old girl after using her for his convenience. The white man is "worshipped" by Cio-Cio San, despite his intentions to leave her, reflecting a sense of White Superiority and American Exceptionalism yet again.

By the end of the opera, it is only Cio-Cio San, the abused, manipulated, and objectified Asian woman of the plot, who commits suicide for the pains Pinkerton has caused through his actions.

The Toll of the Sea, a film from 1922, portrays the very same Madam Butterfly archetype.[22] Anna Mae Wong, one of the first Chinese American actresses in the United States to have mainstream roles, played the role of the "Butterfly" archetype in her character, Lotus Flower. In the film, Lotus Flower rescues an American male named Allen Carver from drowning, subsequently marrying him after falling in love. Similar to the other stories of the Madam Butterfly trope, Carver eventually abandons her in China, returning to his old "normal" life in the United States despite his previous promises to Lotus Flower to take her home with him. Lotus Flower gives birth to Carver's son, naming him Allen after his father. Carver eventually returns to China, accompanied by his American wife, Elsie. After Lotus Flower realizes the situation, she quickly asks Elsie to take her son to the United States with Allen Carver. Heartbroken and left behind, Lotus Flower drowns herself in the same sea from which she initially saved Allen Carver. [23]

In the more well-known and much more recent 1989 Broadway musical *Miss Saigon*, Claude-Michel Schönberg and Alain Boublil rewrote the classic *Madame Butterfly* story, this time depicting an American sergeant and a Vietnamese

---

22   Frances Marion, *Toll of the Sea*. United States: Metro Pictures, 1922.

23   Ibid.

prostitute.[24] Madame Butterfly and Miss Saigon share the same overarching storyline of an Asian woman, this time a prostitute, who falls in love with a soldier, gets pregnant, and is ultimately abandoned by the soldier who takes upon an American wife. Identical to the plots of stories that highlight the Madame Butterfly archetype, the American couple takes the child with them to their home country. The heartbroken, left-behind Vietnamese protagonist commits suicide.[25]

The only difference between the 1904 opera and 1989 musical is that in *Miss Saigon*, the white male is an American sergeant and the Asian woman is a Vietnamese prostitute, whereas in Madame Butterfly, it is a Japanese girl and American Navy lieutenant. The 1989 Broadway musical made just around thirty years before modern day is a prime example of how the extremely narrow-minded and "Orientalist" perspective of Asian women that started in the 1800s continues to persist into modern day, celebrating the history of US military involvement in Asia, the objectification and prostitution of women, and the priority of the white man and white woman's life over the Asian female.

ANTI-MISCEGENATION AND THE YELLOW PERIL

Nineteenth and twentieth-century American history show the origin of the "Dragon Lady." Whereas Victorian men were becoming "entranced" by geishas in Japan in the 1800s, the United States in the late 1800s and 1900s was struggling against "yellow peril," or the fear of Asians disrupting or

---

24   Claude-Michel Schönberg and Alain Boublil. "Miss Saigon." 1989.

25   Ibid.

taking over Western values such as "democracy, Christianity, and technological innovation."[26] Miscegenation, or "marriage, cohabitation, or sexual intercourse between a white person and a member of another race," brought upon a threat to the illusory "homogeneity" of whiteness.[27]

According to William H. Tucker, a Professor of Psychology at Rutgers University-Camden, there have been three different types of scientific explanations that have offered "putative support for racial discrimination" throughout history, all attacking the topic of miscegenation and "interbreeding."[28] One explanation was the belief in the United States and South Africa that "interbreeding" between races brought about biological dangers, eventually leading to miscegenation laws preventing interracial marriages.[29] This claim, mostly derived by mid-nineteenth-century physicians, advocated the idea that "mixed blood, 'mulattoes' were more susceptible to disease than either of their parents."[30] Anthropologists around the time also claimed that "interbreeding" would lead to progressively less fertile and sterile persons.[31]

---

26 "Asian Immigration: The 'Yellow Peril,'" *Race in the United States, 1880-1949 Exhibit: Student Digital Gallery at BGSU*, accessed April 29, 2020.

27 Merriam-Webster, s.v. "miscegenation (n.)," accessed September 28, 2020.

28 William H. Tucker, "The Ideology of Racism: Misusing Science to Justify Racial Discrimination," *United Nations Chronicle*, accessed April 29, 2020.

29 Ibid.

30 Ibid.

31 Ibid.

By the early twentieth century, the rise of genetics led to the idea that marriage between different races would lead to genetic "disharmony." According to Tucker, Charles Benedict Davenport, a famous researcher at the time, claimed "if a member of a tall race... should mate with a member of a small race... their offspring could inherit the genes for large internal organs from one parent and the small stature from the other, resulting in viscera that would be too large for the frame."[32] Although these genetic claims were quickly disproven, social scientists began to claim mixed-race children were "morally and intellectually inferior to either of the parents."[33] Finally, Tucker elaborated on the most common use of science to justify racial discrimination—through perpetuating the idea that certain racial groups are "systematically less well-endowed than others in important cognitive or behavioral traits."[34] Tucker emphasized this claim of lesser moral and intelligent characteristics used throughout history and in the last half-century for oppressive purposes, including to preserve white supremacy in both South Africa and the United States.[35]

As Assistant Professor of English at the United States Naval Academy, Audrey Wu Clark writes, "Anti-miscegenation laws in the United States were not only directed against mixed heritage African Americans but also against Asians after the

---

32 Ibid.
33 Ibid.
34 Ibid.
35 Ibid.

Civil War."[36] This "yellow peril" that perpetuated anti-miscegenation sentiment and xenophobia against Asian Americans in the United States worsened because Chinese laborers often lived in "bachelor societies," increasing the need for sex work in the region.[37]

THE TERRORS OF JOURNALISM

At the time, white journalists singled out Chinese prostitutes, writing stories of the "trafficked yellow slaves" that simultaneously criminalized and victimized the sex workers due to their sexual association with the Chinese laborers.[38] Journalists "racialized discriminatory wages, polygamy, and prostitution as uniquely Chinese 'slave-like' characteristics... to justify race-based discrimination against them."[39]

---

36 Audrey Wu Clark, "Disturbing Stereotypes: Fu Man/ Chan and Dragon Lady Blossoms," *Asian American Literature: Discourse and Pedagogies*, no.3 (2012): 99–118.

37 Iris Chang, *The Chinese in America: A Narrative History* (New York: Penguin Press, 2003).

38 Shauna Lo, "Chinese Women Entering New England: Chinese Exclusion Act Case Files, Boston, 1911-1925," *The New England Quarterly*, no. 3 (2008): 383–409.

39 Diana Lu, "Yang Song and the Long History of Targeting Asian American Sex Workers," *Hyphen Magazine*, August 28, 2019.

Artwork by Janice Khang

Combined with the rising fear and hatred toward the Asian population from the general public, this polarized and defamatory journalism eventually led to the passing of the Anti-Prostitution Act of 1870 in California. The Act stated it was not "lawful, to bring, or land from any ship, boat or vessel, any Mongolian, Chinese or Japanese females... without first presenting to the Commissioner of Immigration evidence satisfactory to him that such female desires voluntarily to come into this State, and is a person of correct habits and good character."[40] In other words, they were given the authority to determine whether or not an Asian woman was "morally corrupt," barring anyone they deemed otherwise.

40　"Anti-Prostitution Act: Chapter CCXXX," Chinatown San Francisco, accessed May 25, 2020.

The idea of "morally corrupt" Asian women was again perpetuated by the Page Act of 1875 to disallow the entry of Asian "forced laborers" and sex workers from entering into the United States.[41] Essentially, however, Chinese female immigrants—whether wives or sex workers, trafficked or not—were deemed Chinese prostitutes by Congressman Horace F. Page, the American politician who represented the Californian district where many Chinese immigrants and laborers resided.[42],56 As Chinese women were generalized to be prostitutes and seen as extremely treacherous and sexual beings in this time period, the media began to exemplify this sentiment in movies and literature—thus birthing the "Dragon Lady" trope in literature and film. With the combination of sexually exploitative journalism and governmental laws that not only generalized Asian women to be prostitutes but also condemned Asian female sex workers, remnants of that legacy can still be seen today in modern day sex work, pornography, film, and literature.

Unfortunately, the anti-miscegenation and "yellow peril" sentiment did not stop here. The country's animosity against the Chinese began to grow against other Asian immigrants after the Chinese Exclusion Act of 1882, when the United States implemented an immigration law that excluded Chinese laborers from immigrating to the United States.[43]

---

41 US Congress, "The Page Act of 1875 (Immigration Act)," 43rd Cong, sess. 2, approved March 3rd, 1875.

42 Ibid.

43 "Chinese Exclusion Act," The African American Policy Forum, accessed April 29, 2020.

In response, the nation started "importing" Japanese men for their cheap labor. Japanese laborers again became feared in a similar fashion to the Chinese laborers as "the cheapness of that labor is likewise a menace to American labor."[44] Japanese immigrants tried to avoid this animosity by attempting to "assimilate" to white values; unfortunately, as history tends to repeat itself, their efforts to assimilate were seen with hostility and led the government to establish the Gentleman's Agreement of 1907, consequently banning Japanese immigration from this point forward.[45] The only exception to this ban was for family reunification, encouraging "Japanese bachelors in America to start families via arranged marriages with women in Japan, whom they met through photos, called 'picture brides.'"[46]

White journalists subsequently began claiming these "picture brides" were victims of trafficking. The combination of anti-Japanese sentiment and concern about the status of "picture brides" eventually led to the Ladies Agreement of 1921 that banned picture brides and immigration from Japan.[47] As Japan had annexed Korea around the time, both Japanese and Korean immigrants and refugees were affected.

---

44 US Congress, *United States Congressional Serial Se Vol. 5864* (Washington, DC: US Government Printing Office, *1911*) 167–170.

45 "Gentlemen's Agreement," History, last modified August 21, 2018.

46 Younho Oh, "Korean Picture Brides in Hawaii: Historical and Literary Narratives," *Journal of Literature and Art Studies*, no. 12 (2017): 1632–1644.

47 Pyong Gap Min, *Asian Americans: Contemporary Trends and Issues* (Pine Forge Press, 2006), 148–152.

Artwork by Claire Cai

This problematic portrayal of Asian women still exists in modern journalism today. For example, in the infamous article "The Case of Jane Doe Ponytail" published in the *New York Times* in 2018, journalists Dan Barry and Jeffrey E. Singer depict Yang Song, an immigrant sex worker killed during a police raid in Queens, in an extremely sexual light.[48] Writer and comedian Diana Lu writes in 2019, "Barry and Singer pore over the lurid details of Song's death with exoticizing, sensationalist language, calling Flushing, Queens, a "netherworld … where sex is sold beside cloudy tanks of fish and crab."[49] They describe residents using exploitative, Orientalist tropes, painting the Asian women Song associated with as pitiful victims and the Asian men as "shifty-eyed, lecherous johns and pimps."[50] Other examples of articles

---

48 Diana Lu, "Yang Song and the Long History of Targeting Asian American Sex Workers," *Hyphen Magazine*, August 28, 2019.

49 Dan Barry and Jeffrey E. Singer, "The Case of Jane Doe Ponytail," *The New York Times,* October 16, 2018.

50 Ibid.

with "poor journalistic integrity" include the *Daily Mail's* article in 2018 on a man who fatally abused his Thai wife. The article included unnecessary photos of the victim in her swimsuit, which distracted the main focus of the heinous crime. Another one of *Daily Mail's* report on a man who murdered his Filipino wife highlighted that such an event happened so that he could go on "a Thai sex holiday," crudely including unrelated photos of Thai pole dancers in the article.[51],[52]

Journalists' focus throughout the 1800s and the early 1900s on the "threat" of Asians, with a specific focus on the sex worker industry and the mischaracterization of Asian women as prostitutes and immoral women, had a major impact on US immigration and its laws around the Southeast Asian communities. The perspective that journalists created and promoted of Asians, and especially Asian women, still persists today. Comprehensive narratives have been erased for sexually exploitative exposure, shifting the focus from these women and their humanity to more of their attractiveness and sexuality—a commodity that "sells." For hundreds of years, the same practice of how Asian women, and especially East and Southeast Asian women, are portrayed in a sexual light, continue in the realm of journalism.

---

51 Iain Burns, "British Man Is Arrested for 'Kicking His Thai Wife to Death When She Refused to Have Sex with Him,'" *Daily Mail*, April 16, 2018.

52 Allan Hall, "German Man Admits Killing His Filipino Wife and Slicing Her Body into Eight Pieces So He Could Go on a Sex Holiday to Thailand," *Daily Mail*, October 26, 2016.

WHITE SEXUAL IMPERIALISM

With the permeation of these sexual stereotypes regarding Asian and Asian American women, a much darker, insidious theme can be found in these corners of history: white sexual imperialism. White sexual imperialism, as Sunny Woan's journal excerpt in the *Washington and Lee Journal of Civil Rights and Social Justice* defines, refers to the "sexual gender dynamic" that "involves a white male and a non-white female" where "the non-white female descends from a culture or community that has been historically colonized by European or Anglican nations."[53] This concept derives from Orientalism and the subjugation of Asia by Western powers, namely the United States.

Rudyard Kipling's "White Man's Burden," a term he used in his poem regarding American colonial rule in the Philippines, is a perfect example of the imperialist mindset the United States and other Western powers had when colonizing areas of Asia—the burden to dominate and subjugate for the betterment of these societies and the people.[54] This justification objectified Asia as a whole, both removing its voice and viewing its people as conquests for the overall good of humanity. In that process, women also became nothing but sexual objects; taken over, raped, and sexually conquered. Their overall humanity became irrelevant and the justification of the white man's gruesome, sexual domination of

---

53 Sunny Woan, "White Sexual Imperialism: A Theory of Asian Feminist Jurisprudence," *Wash. & Lee Journal of Civil Rights & Social Justice* 14, no. 2 (2008): 275–301.

54 Rudyard Kipling, "The White Man's Burden," February 12, 1899.

these women as objects came to be seen as consensual on the women's part to perpetuate overall imperialist justification.

Exhibited throughout multiple aspects of American history are elements of white sexual imperialism. For example, in the Philippines American War between 1899–1902, women and girls were often viewed as sexual objects existing to be conquered, ridiculed, and used.[55] The United States maintained a relatively condescending outlook toward the Philippines, evident as President McKinley, the president during the United States' conquest of the Philippines, argument that Filipinos were "incapable of self-government."[56] During the US colonial rule of the Philippines from 1898 to 1946, William H. Taft, who at the time was the American Governor-General of the Philippines, stated in a similar statement that the civilians, or whom he coined, "little brown brothers," would need "fifty or one hundred years of close supervision 'to develop anything resembling Anglo-Saxon political principles and skills.'"[57] US sailors then used this very same condescending outlook and the "little brown brothers" saying to sexualize the women, calling them "little brown fucking machines powered by rice"—a popular saying eventually printed upon

55 "The Philippine American War, 1899-1902," Department of State Office of the Historian, accessed June 10, 2020.

56 "The Philippines, 1989-1946," History, Art, & Archives United States House of Representatives, accessed June 10, 2020.

57 Spencer C. Tucker, *The Encyclopedia of the Spanish American and Philippine American Wars: A Political, Social, and Military History* (ABC-CLIO, 2009), 478.

T-shirts for sale.[58] These women were viewed as conquered, dehumanized objects who could be ridiculed and used.

Along the lines of white sexual imperialism came the further perpetration of the Lotus Blossom stereotype combined with the continuation of the Madame Butterfly archetype. With WWII, American soldiers began to encounter East Asian women overseas and in local bars and in the form of geishas. The rise of the "geisha" and "Lotus Blossom" stereotype of subservient and domestic Asian women thus once again enforced during this time. Not only were American soldiers simply encountering these women, but they were abusing them through coerced prostitution under a deal with the Japanese government.[59]

According to an Associated Press review of historical documents from World War II after Japan's surrender, the Japanese government, with US occupation authorities' tacit approval, permitted an official brothel system forcing the women involved to participate. Eric Talmadge, the Associated Press's North Korea Bureau Chief, states, "Tens of thousands of women were employed to provide cheap sex to US troops until the spring of 1946, when General MacArthur shut the brothels down."[60] The Ibaraki Prefectural Police Department's official accounts show that police had to "set up sexual comfort stations for the occupation troops," in an

---

58   Aida F. Santos, *Gathering the Dust: The Base Issue in the Philippines*, (New York: The New Press, 1992), 40.

59   Eric Talmadge, "GIs Frequented Japans' 'Comfort Women,'" *The Washington Post*, April 25, 2007.

60   Ibid.

attempt to "create a breakwater to protect regular women and girls" through the "special work of experienced women."[61] Policemen and Tokyo businessmen established brothels under the supervision of the Recreation and Amusement Association (RAA).[62]

According to Seiichi Kaburagi, the chief of public relations for the Recreation and Amusement Association (RAA), GIs would pay upright for tickets and condoms; they would then enter what was called the "Komachien" or "The Babe Garden" that held thirty-eight women, eventually increased to one hundred.[63] Records show each "woman serviced from fifteen to sixty clients a day."[64] According to Kaburagi's memoirs, which were published after the occupation ended in 1952, many of the comfort women were coerced to join brothels due to the demand of brothel operators coercing inexperienced girls as prostitutes and because of the financial strain on their families.[65] He wrote about Takita, a nineteen-year old girl whose relatives had been killed in the war and had responded "to an ad seeking an office worker."[66] Instead of an office worker, she was forced to become a prostitute for these brothels.

According to a 1945 memorandum from Lt. McDonald, it was clear the United States occupation forces were aware of the

---

61 Ibid.

62 Ibid.

63 Ibid.

64 Ibid.

65 Ibid.

66 Ibid.

forced prostitution occurring in these brothels.[67] He stated, "The girl is impressed into contracting by the desperate financial straits of her parents and their urging, occasionally supplemented by her willingness to make such a sacrifice to help her family."[68] It is the belief of our informants, however, that in urban districts, the practice of enslaving girls, while much less prevalent than in the past, still exists.

Due to complaints from military chaplains and the spread of sexually transmitted diseases among US troops, General MacArthur made all brothels and places of prostitution off-limits for the troops in 1946.[69] Dr. Yuki Tanaka, a professor at the Hiroshima Peace Institute, states that by this time, more than "a quarter of all American GIs in the occupation forces had a sexually transmitted disease."[70] "The sudden off-limits policy put more than 150,000 Japanese women out of jobs," Tanaka writes in his 2002 book *Japan's Comfort Women: Sexual Slavery and Prostitution During World War II and the US Occupation*, forcing them to continue working in sexual slavery to help with their family's financial strains.[71]

---

67 Eric Talmadge, "US Troops Used Japan Brothels after WWII," *The Seattle Times,* April 26, 2007.

68 Ibid.

69 Eric Talmadge, "GIs Frequented Japans' 'Comfort Women,'" *The Washington Post,* April 25, 2007.

70 Associated Press, "US Troops Used Japanese Brothels after WWII," *Asia-Pacific NBC News,* April 27, 2007.

71 Yuki Tanaka and Toshiyuki Tanaka, *Japan's Comfort Women: Sexual Slavery and Prostitution During World War II and the US Occupation,* (Psychology Press, 2002).

A similar situation of coerced prostitution and the objectification of Asian women is visible in South Korea. According to David Vine, an associate professor of Anthropology at American University in Washington, DC and his book, *Base Nation: How US Military Bases Abroad Harm America and the World*, US military authorities, who were occupying Korea after World War II, took over a number of the comfort stations in Korea that initially ran under Japanese authority.[72] As the Japanese military had forced hundreds of thousands of women from "Korea, China, Okinawa, and rural Japan and other parts of Asia into sexual slavery, providing soldiers with 'royal gifts' from the emperor," US authorities continued the operation of these comfort stations, providing extremely dire conditions for the women involved.[73]

After the US signed the Korea-US Mutual Defense Treaty in 1953, camp towns became extremely popular. According to Katherine Moon, a Professor in the Department of Political Science at Wellesley College, camp towns were "deeply stigmatized twilight zones" having an "estimated 300,000 sex workers."[74] During this time, many of the soldiers "owned" some of the girls in a system of cohabitation. Men would have a small house and furniture and their own "concubine," which they could sell to the next man as they left to return to the United States.[75]

---

72 David Vine, *Base Nation: How US Military Bases Abroad Harm America and the World*, (Henry Holt and Company, 2015).

73 Ibid.

74 David Vine, "My Body Was Not Mine, but the US Military's," *Politico*, November 3, 2015.

75 Ibid.

Once again, a similar pattern is apparent with US military involvement in the Vietnam War. Numerous rapes and sexual atrocities were committed by American soldiers at this time, permeating this idea of conquering women's bodies yet again. For example, in the infamous My Lai massacre, over 500 unarmed civilians, including women and children, were massacred by a company of American soldiers.[76] Before their deaths, records indicate the women and young girls were first raped and tortured by the soldiers.[77]

Additionally, numerous US military bases stationed in Thailand at this time, where American soldiers frequently participated in engaging with sex workers as a part of the authority-organized "Rest and Recreation" leave.[78] Dr. Porphant Ouyyanont, an Associate Professor at the Sukhothai Thammathirat Open University writes that in 1966, "there were at least 652 night clubs, bars, and massage parlors in the whole country of which 336 were in Bangkok, 126 were in the five provinces housing US bases in the northeast, and 190 in the other provinces particularly close to the two bases in provinces in the central region."[79] This again cemented the concept that Asian women were "hypersexual" and "easy" beings, as American men were not only raping and "conquering" civilians during war in the most inhumane, objectified

76 Quang Ngai, "Unidentified Vietnamese Women and Children in My Lai."
    Vintage Everyday, March 16, 2018.

77 Ibid.

78 Porphant Ouyyanont, "The Vietnam War and Tourism in Bangkok's Development, 1960-70," *Southeast Asian* Studies 39, no. 2 (January 2001):1–33.

79 Ibid.

manners, they were also engaging with sex workers who were often forced into prostitution due to financial needs.

The remnants of this white sexual imperialism bled into both Asian countries and the United States even after the wars ended. A study by the University of Ottowa in 2017 found there are currently five times more commercial sex workers in Thailand near former US bases than unused Thai bases, with its sex industry most likely to have developed due to an agricultural crisis and the demand for financial support.[80] This Oriental justification of systems of sex work developed during the times of war were the roots in enforcing pre-existing stereotypes regarding Asian women and enforcing red-light districts in Asia, especially in the Southeast region where much sex tourism exists today.

UNRAVELING THE REMNANTS

This concept that Asian women are "willing to be raped," "submissive," and "hypersexual" was a byproduct of the West's "use" of Asian women as sex objects on and around Asian US military bases, a horrific and dehumanized set of stereotypes that exist to this day.

For example, qualitative analysis by Bitna Kim found that many non-Asian males held positive stereotypes of Asian women as "intelligent, educated, successful, family-oriented,

---

80 Abel Brodeur, Warn N Lekfuangfu, and Yanos Zylberberg, "War, Migration and the Origins of the Thai Sex Industry," *University of Ottawa*, no. 1 (Spring 2017): 1–57.

and beautiful."[81] However, she also noted that most of the interviewees stated Asian women were "submissive" in one way or another, some even saying, "Women serve the men... they do things for him that the Western culture has long forgotten."[82]

Another study by Dr. Shruti Mukkamala and Dr. Karen L. Suyemoto analyzed 107 participants, all of whom were Asian women, with only four of the participants stating they had never experienced any form of discrimination.[83] The other 103 participants experienced discrimination divided into fifteen types, with six being specific to race and gender interactions. These six types were discriminatory actions that assumed these women to be: exotic (objectified and exoticized), not a leader (incapable), submissive (quiet, passive), cute and small (visual expectations), invisible (lacking voice), and to be service workers (working at a low-level gendered job).[84]

The remnants of such history have left its marks upon society in different ripples. For some, the mark was left in the form of blatant objectification and infantilization tied upon their skin color. For example, when I interviewed individual Shi,

---

81 Bitna Kim, "Asian Female and Caucasian Male Couples: Exploring the Attraction," *Pastoral Psychology* 60, no. 2 (Spring 2011): 233–244.

82 Ibid.

83 Shruti Mukkamala and Karen L. Suyemoto, "Racialized Sexism/Sexualized Racism: A Multimethod Study of Intersectional Experiences of Discrimination for Asian American Women," *Asian American Journal of Psychology* 9, no. 1 (Spring 2018): 32–46.

84 Ibid.

a recent college graduate from Arkansas, she told me that she had multiple experiences of meeting guys who would blatantly tell her they were attracted to her "submissive" and "cute" character. She also had an ex-boyfriend complain to her that he stayed with her solely for her Asian ethnicity.

For others, it left perceptions of modern-day colonialism and cultural appropriation. To give an example, a Filipino-Canadian interviewee reported that she had known a classmate fixated on living out a fantasy of "being Filipino." He was obsessively addicted to adopting the Filipino culture, whether through going to the Philippines, learning Tagalog, or only wanting to date Filipino women. For her, his actions were a direct reminder of the colonization of the Philippines, making her feel not only degraded, but extremely unsafe.

As seen by these interviewees' experiences, there is a very real, insidious pain that follows the remnants of history into modern-day society. From the famous literature and Broadway plots perpetuating the Madame Butterfly archetype to remnants of white sexual imperialism following US military involvement in Asia came the insidious stereotypes that have painted Asian women in a hypersexual and submissive light. It is not simply a preference or a joke to indicate one's belief that an Asian woman is attractive due to her submissive nature or sexually appealing light—it is the subconscious or conscious belief and projection of years of war atrocities and subjugation that occurred developing into these stereotypes. Although seemingly harmless, this sexualization of Asian females, so prevalently seen in media and the terrible sexual pick-up lines Asian females receive has a dark history often forgotten in our history books.

For the longest time, I felt like a loser because I was Asian. I was less of a man. Less successful. I was unattractive.

Worthless.

—ANONYMOUS MALE INTERVIEWEE
IN HIS EARLY TWENTIES

CHAPTER 4

"MASCULINITY"

———

[Begin Transcript 00:00:10]

Beep.

"Okay, the recording has started. Whenever you're ready."

"Sounds good. I'm ready now."

"Can you tell me about your experience growing up in the United States as an Asian American guy?"

"[Laughs] Where do I even start. Hmmm... So I grew up under really, really traditional Asian parents. You know, where the male child was extremely preferable. It was even more emphasized for me because I was the first male child of the first male child—if that makes sense."

"Oh, so your dad was the first male child of his family?"

"Mhm. So because he had grown up in a traditional family that also emphasized this form of 'favoritism' toward the man, we were both instilled with the idea of having to be the 'masculine' figure in the household from an early age."

"That sounds like a lot of pressure. What was that like?"

"Well, there was a weird power dynamic for sure. My grandfather always had this favoritism toward me over my siblings. I was also raised with the idea that I had to 'be a man' and to become like this stone wall of stability that could never cry.

"Mmm… I see. That must have been hard."

[00:01:36]

"Yeah, it was hard. I mean, all elements of toxic masculinity are you know, toxic. But it was also just hard because there seemed to be this weird dichotomy between my life at home and in society in general."

"Can you elaborate more on that?"

"Well, I began to realize, like you know, on television, there would only be the Asian Kung Fu dude or the weird nerd dude. They were always the side character, the butt of a joke, or some weird Master Sensei guy. And at school, I remember from a young age my friends would joke around that 'as an Asian male, you're only acceptably allowed to date an Asian female because non-Asian females won't find you attractive in the first place, so don't even attempt it in the first place.'"

"Really?"

"Yeah… and I couldn't help but believe it because, in high school, there were more relationships of Asian females with non-Asian males, but not vice versa. I don't know if it's okay to say this, but it just felt like Asian females were *allowed* into white culture, whereas the men weren't."

"I see. Did you find yourself sticking more to your Asian peers then? And can you tell me more about this dichotomy you mentioned earlier?"

"… I don't know. It was just weird to constantly be spoon-fed this toxic masculinity all my life by my family where I had to 'be a man,' but the minute I stepped foot outside my house, it seemed like no one was going to 'see me like a man.' If you wanted to be treated like a man, whatever that means, you had to be in an Asian circle. If I could never see any elements of a 'masculine' and 'attractive' Asian man on television or in real life, how was I supposed to magically convince myself that I was exactly that?"

"Mmmm…"

"And of course, there was this weird thing with the whole small penis stereotype. I never even thought about it until high school, but for some reason, it began to be emphasized by my peers as I got older. Like, those around me began attributing their masculinities to the size of their penises— especially in the locker rooms for my swim team. It was of course, offensive, but it didn't directly affect me as much because I wasn't sexually active. For my Asian peers that were though, I could see how much it hurt their confidence and self-esteem."

Beep.

[End Transcript 00:05:26]

Interview with Zhang, Chinese American man in his late twenties.

***

FEEDING A LIE

If you've ever lived in a country with a dominantly white population like the United States, or you're relatively familiar with any form of Western media, you're probably aware of the "Asian men have small penises" stereotype—or the stereotype that Asian men have smaller-than-average penises.

Simply searching "Asian Penis" on Urban Dictionary, one can easily find offensive and demeaning definitions like "The smallest dick on the planet" or "a very tiny unit of measurement, approximately 1/5 the width of a human hair."[85] You can also easily find references to this offensive stereotype in famous Hollywood movies like the *Hangover 2,* where three white protagonists find a passed out Ken Jeong and play with his "tiny mushroom dick."[86] A few years back, ESPN columnist, Whitlock, even received the spotlight for offensively tweeting about Chinese American NBA player Jeremy Lin

---

85 Urban Dictionary., s.v. "Asian Penis," accessed April 6, 2020.

86 Todd Phillips, Dan Goldberg, Craig Mazin, and Scot Armstrong, *The Hangover Part II.* United States: Warner Bros., 2011.

and how a lucky lady was going to "feel a couple of inches of pain tonight."[87]

Like Zhang mentioned in the interview I had with him, Asian men are often portrayed as the "Kung Fu" guy or as the "geeky" nerd, neither of which depicts Asian men as a prominent masculine force in mainstream media. From classic chick flick movies like *Sixteen Candles* where characters like Long Duk Dong, an undesirable foreign student, uncomfortably flirts with the white and beautiful Molly Ringwald, to modern-day BBC's "Chinese Burn" where characters like Huang Lo, an unattractive, small-penis carrying racist, continue to exist, Asian males are often equated to negligible side-characters.[88],[89]

Deemed throughout the media as "unattractive," Asian men often deal with demeaning and offensive stereotypes. Prominent comedian Amy Schumer exemplified this offensiveness quite effectively during an interview on the *Howard Stern Show*, where she explained how her parents would probably be mad if she brought an Asian guy home, saying they would probably state "I don't understand... do you really want to fuck this guy?"[90] Comedians like Greg Wilson often liked

87 Bill Hanstock, "Jason Whitlock 'Congratulates' Jeremy Lin With Racist Tweet," *SB Nation Bay Area*, last modified February 11, 2012.

88 *Sixteen Candles*. United States: Universal Pictures Channel Productions, 1984.

89 *Chinese Burn*. BBC, November 27, 2017.

90 "Amy Schumer Makes Offensive, Arguably Racist Comment About Asian Men," The Howard Stern Show, uploaded on March 12, 2017, YouTube video, 0:00:58.

to start their stand-up routines with lines like "Isn't it weird the way everybody wants to bang an Asian chick, but nobody wants to date an Asian dude."[91] Even the other day as I was binge-watching *Dexter*, a popular crime TV show from 2013, I was able to notice the only Asian male was a Japanese American character named Masuka who played an unattractive, yet hypersexual and perverted role that the series often made fun of.[92]

"Attractiveness is a very haphazard dish that can't be boiled down to height or skin color, but Asian men are told that regardless of what the idyllic mirepoix is or isn't, we just don't have the ingredients."

—TELEVISION HOST EDDIE HUANG[93]

But that was it. A "joke" on a comedy special. A "humorous" phenomenon.

91   "Asian Men Have Small Penises-Asian Small Dick Jokes-Stand-up Comedy!" Comic Comedy, uploaded on April 15, 2013, YouTube video, 0:00:03.

92   *Dexter.* Showtime, October 1, 2006.

93   Eddie Huang, "Hey, Steve Harvey, Who Says I Might Not Steal Your Girl?" *The New York Times,* January 14, 2017.

It was a "funny reality" we accepted, never questioning how problematic it was to generalize and depict the body parts and attraction level of Asian men of the diaspora. A sentiment I feel that we, as a society, simply accepted, never really knowing where or why this stereotype existed or where it had originated. But why?

How had we allowed such traumatizing objectification for Asian men to be so easily normalized? Why was the media so intent on depicting Asian men in a humorous, nonattractive way? Why did it seem that Asian men were so widely rejected despite the fetishization of Asian women? How were the two interconnected?

***

CHASING THE FACTS

To begin, I wanted to research this "small penis" stereotype. I mean, how could I study this topic without finding the roots of such a pervasive stereotype so normalized within not only my life but in society? It seemed to be the defining characteristic of how Asian men were often made fun of in mainstream media. Growing up, my guy friends had often conversed about reading a new study on global penis sizes and standards across countries, so I was sure there was *something* out there that I could obtain information from.

Despite the popularity of such a pervasive stereotype, I came to the shocking conclusion there was not a *single* credible source or research study backing up this horrendous stereotype. The data I came upon was mostly self-reported data with extremely high voluntary response bias. The data from these studies ranged from data portraying Korean and Japanese men to have the smallest penises in the world, to studies showing them to have larger-than American penises on an average basis.

For example, Mandatory.com once uploaded an infographic of a cross-section of global penis size using preexisting surveys and data from different sites.[94] In their "Red" section depicting the smallest penis sizes from 3.8–4.6 inches, it included the countries of China, India, Indonesia, Japan, North Korea, South Korea, Malaysia, Philippines, Singapore, Taiwan, Thailand, and Vietnam.[95] Nevertheless, taking a brief second to analyze its methodology revealed this data to be based on self-measurement and self-reporting—an extremely unreliable source for something considered *objective* "global data."

Despite the lack of credible data, I did find many news sources quoting this inaccurate data and using it to promote some form of "research discovery" that there were indeed penis size differences across ethnicities. It was also extremely common to find inquiries on community-sourced questionnaire websites like Yahoo! Answers, where users would ask the internet whether or not Asian men really had the smallest penises. The majority of the replies wrote that they indeed had the smallest penises because that was their portrayal in pornography—the biggest penises were always from Black

---

94   Matt Branham, "Which Country Has the Biggest Dicks in the World?" *Mandatory*, February 26, 2015.

95   Ibid.

men or Indigenous men, according to these responses. Again, the basis of these responses was on the perceptions of penises by individuals who likely had no actual knowledge or experience interacting with an Asian penis.

As I continued my research, I came upon the concept of "race realism," the forefront "researchers" permeating such toxic ideologies. Advocates of "race realism" influenced these studies and "anecdotes," believing there were real and pervasive differences between racial groups in personality, intelligence, and social behavior. These individuals believed these differences to have a "genetic and evolutionary origin," and that they could explain "disparities in important social and economic outcomes between races."[96] One of the most prominent figures in such racist field was J. Philippe Rushton, a heavy advocate of race realism who "proposed that the major races can be sorted into a human hierarchy based on their supposed reproductive strategies."[97]

Rushton's theories, which are said to have flourished in the '80s, included the r-K life history theory, or the theory that there is a dichotomy of reproductive strategies: the r-strategy that involves minimal investment for a larger number of offspring and the k-strategy that involves greater investment

---

96 Scott McGreal, "The Pseudoscience of Race Differences in Penis Size," *Psychology Today*. Sussex Publishers, October 16, 2012.

97 J. Philippe Rushton & Anthony F. Bogaert, "Race Differences in Sexual Behavior: Testing an Evolutionary Hypothesis," *Journal of Research in Personality 21*, no. 21, (December 1987): 529–551.

for fewer offspring.[98] He argued that Africans were the most r-selected, whereas Asians were the most K-selected.[99]

White Europeans? Perfectly in between.

Rushton used these claims to argue reproductive strategies were tied to mental and physical characteristics, thus making African men having the smallest brains and the largest penises, while Asian men had the largest brain and smaller penises. **White European men were the "perfect" middle.**[100]

Although this sounds like racism-based science from a lifetime ago, just in 2012, a similar study by Richard Lynn claimed to have found "evidence" there are indeed differences in penis size based on their different races.[101] Lynn, similar to Rushton, argued there was this "middle" ground in European and American individuals. Lynn built on earlier work by Rushton using an argument that there are differences in penis size based on lower levels of testosterone in European and Asian men than Africans.[102] His source? Widosky and Greene's study from 1940 studied the effects of sex hormones on **rat penises.**[103]

---

98 Ibid.

99 Ibid.

100 Ibid.

101 Richard Lynn, "Rushton's r–K Life History Theory of Race Differences in Penis Length and Circumference Examined in 113 Populations," *Personality and Individual Differences* 55, no. 3, (July 2013): 261–266.

102 Ibid.

103 H.S. Wigodsky and R.R. Greene, "The Effect of Testosterone, Estrone, and Estradiol Applied Locally to the Penis of the Rat," *Endocrinology*

Overall, the stereotype of the "small penis" trope pertains to the historical viewing of Asian men as "effeminate" beings, their bodies reduced to pure objectification. By objectifying men to solely their penis size, Asian men were inherently labeled as too effeminate and submissive in comparison to "perfect" white men, the "norm" that Asian men fail to match up to. In other words, Asian men, the submissive and desexualized beings, and Black men, the hypersexual and aggressive beings, were on the two ends of a spectrum that aimed to maintain the concept that the white body was the "perfect balance" of masculinity and sexual appeal, an extremely oppressive method of ethnic body policing that marginalizes minority bodies for not conforming to the white ideal.

In other words, despite the lack of actual scientific or academic data to back up this stereotype, researchers were often very intent on confirming that Asian men had small penises, for one reason or another. This sparked my curiosity even more, as it seemed it was not only researchers who were very intent—no, *are still* intent, in promoting this idea that white European bodies are the perfect "middle ground" between the "beastly" Black men and the "effeminate" Asian men. They couldn't have been the only influencers in society to normalize such racism on such a widespread level.

How did such a mentality form? More importantly, how did it spread in such a pervasive, normalized way to the corners of society?

26, no. 6, (June 1940): 1078–1080.

THE FEMINIZATION OF ASIAN MEN

Ever since the first Chinese communities started immigrating to the United States during the 1850s in search of escaping economic chaos in China with the California Gold Rush, the immigration of unskilled, cheap Chinese American labor, or "coolie" labor, was accepted and encouraged on the Western front.[104],[105] Chinese laborers were seen as less demanding than white workers and were preferred by many industries due to their cheap labor, considered an essential part in helping developing industries in the area. For example, the Central Pacific Railroad was able to purchase these laborers for two-thirds the price of white workers, using the cheap labor to complete the Western portion of the transcontinental railroad required by the government.[106],[107] However, this encouragement of labor soon turned into anti-Chinese sentiment as the Chinese immigrants again were seen as a threat to the white homogeneity of the society.

104 Sucheng Chan, *Entry Denied: Exclusion and the Chinese Community in America 1882-1943* (1990).

105 Michael Park, "Asian American Masculinity Eclipsed: A Legal and Historical Perspective of Emasculation Through US Immigration Practices," *The Modern American* 8, no. 1, (2013).

106 Mary R. Coolidge, *Chinese Immigration* (1909) (New York City, Holt & Company, 1909).

107 Ronald Takaki, *Strangers from a Different Shore: A History of Asian Americans* (New York City, Little, Brown and Company, 1989).

Photograph by Eileene Lee

This resentment and threat to "racial purity" led to legal and governmental policies directly or indirectly targeting Chinese immigrants, such as the Nationality Act of 1870, that deliberately disallowed Chinese, despite including Native and African Americans, the right to citizenship.[108] By 1878, in the infamous *In re Ah Yup* court ruling, Chinese immigrants were dictated to be ineligible for American citizenship because of their non-white ethnicity.[109]

By 1882, as previously mentioned, anti-Chinese sentiment rose to include the Chinese Exclusion Act, the first

---

108 "Naturalization Act of 1870," Immigration History, accessed August 21, 2020.

109 "In re Ah Yup Rules Chinese Ineligible for Naturalized Citizenship on April 29, 1878," Smithsonian Asian Pacific American Center, April 8, 2010.

immigration law excluding an entire ethnic group.[110] By the 1900s, despite the xenophobic laws already implemented in response to the anti-Chinese sentiment in the white community, xenophobic sentiment combined with white superiority rose once again with the United States' involvement in the Spanish American War and its other military agendas. Congress passed the Immigration Act of 1924, limiting the number of immigrants allowed entry into the United States based on national origins quota.[111] The Magnuson Act passed by Congress in 1943 granted Chinese immigrants the ability to naturalize and become accepted as American citizens.[112]

---

110 "Chinese Exclusion Act," *History.com*, A&E Television Networks, last modified August 24, 2018.

111 "The Immigration Act of 1924 (The Johnson-Reed Act)," US Department of State Office of The Historian, accessed on March 23, 2020.

112 "Repeal of the Chinese Exclusion Act, 1943," US Department of State Office of The Historian, accessed on March 23, 2020.

Photograph by Eileene Lee

The naturalization and immigration laws sparked from the xenophobic "yellow peril" depicted Asian immigrants, especially Asian male laborers, as emasculated "lesser" beings. In other words, the debilitated capacities of Asian immigrants in becoming citizens represented much more than the overlying removal of political representation. According to social theorists, the idea of citizenship in the United States depended on the patriarchal household and this concept of rationalized masculinity.[113] Asian men, being denied the right to be a citizen in the United States, were thus denied their "masculinity" and male identity. Asian men, compared to white and non-Asian males given the capability to naturalize as American citizens, were denied the ability to be

---

113 R.W. Connell, *Gender and Power; Society, the Person and Sexual Politics* (Redwood City: Stanford University Press, 1987).

dictated under the law as a "male" until 1943's Magnuson Act.[114] Additionally, as mentioned in the previous chapter, exclusion laws and anti-miscegenation laws disallowed Asian females from entering Asian communities, emasculating the Chinese laborer men through restricting their access to heterosexual norms and familial ideals at the time.

In addition, the 1922 Cable Act implemented a system where any female citizen of the country would lose their citizenship if they married an "alien ineligible to citizenship."[115] Since Asian men were deemed ineligible for naturalization until 1943, for a multitude of years, women were influenced by the law to view Asian men as "effeminate" and "other" beings in the United States. [116]

On top of all this, Asian males were often laborers in typically "female" workplaces in society. This included the food industry, the tailoring industry, and perhaps the most evident at the time, the laundry industry.[117] This was due to the unfortunate reality that in other labor-based industries such as the mining and factory industries, Asian laborers were often abused and violently attacked in response to xenophobic rhetoric. As there was also a shortage of women, especially in the Asian-based areas, Chinese men often turned to self-employment. They began to work in positions typically associated with women.[118] This even furthered the

---

114 "Magnuson Act," *Britannica*, accessed on March 24, 2020.

115 "Cable Act of 1922," Immigration History, accessed on March 26, 2020.

116 Ibid.

117 Ibid.

118 Ibid.

concretization of Asian males as feminine beings in society, permeating this thought to placate the xenophobic fear held by the white homogeneity that Asian males could "take" or "corrupt" their women and their jobs.

MEDIA AND STEREOTYPES

As history often portrayed Asian men as feminine beings, lesser than white males in their perpetual "otherness," emphasizing painting male femininity in a negative light, Hollywood responded by portraying Asian men under a similar sexually emasculating light. According to Richard Fung, a queer activist, writer, and Professor at OCAD University, since at least the 1920s, "Asian men have been represented as the 'egghead/wimp,' or—in what may be analogous to the lotus blossom-dragon lady dichotomy—'the kung fu master/ninja/samurai.' He is sometimes dangerous, sometimes friendly, but almost always characterized by a desexualized Zen asceticism."[119]

There are countless other examples in the history of Western media. From Charlie Chan, the "neutered and servile" detective from the 1920s to 1980s, Fu Manchu, the predatory evil mastermind, to the thick accented and bucktoothed Mr. Yunioshi in the 1961 hit *Breakfast at Tiffany's* (who Mickey

---

119 Richard Fung, "Looking for My Penis: The Eroticized Asian in Gay Video Porn," (1991).

Rooney yellowfaced), Hollywood is sprinkled with racist remnants of Asian male portrayal.[120],[121],[122]

As Fung describes in his powerful essay, "Looking for My Penis," Asian men have a completely different story to the often fantasized and sexualized Asian women. Asian women have existed (and still exist) in film as "passive figures who exist to serve men—as love interests for white men" without any love relationships between "Asian women and Asian men."[123] This is apparent in movies with any form of inter-racial romance that involves an Asian individual; it is *always* a romance between an Asian woman and a white man (or non-Asian man).

When analyzing films that simply take place in Asia, such as *The Last Samurai* or even the Netflix film, *The Outsider,* one can easily see that white males are the only ones that fall in love with the Asian woman—never the Asian man.[124],[125] Frankly speaking, an Asian man rarely falls in love with *any* woman in a mutual, romantic manner. Even in the her-alded film *To All the Boys I've Loved Before,* the storyline inherently circles around an Asian American female chasing after the ideal white man, subsequently advocating for white

---

120 *Charlie Chan's Secret*, United States: 20th Century Fox Studios, 1936.

121 *The Face of Fu Manchu*, Hallam Production, 1965.

122 *Breakfast at Tiffany's*, United States: Paramount Pictures, 1961.

123 Richard Fung, "Looking for My Penis: The Eroticized Asian in Gay Video Porn," (1991).

124 *The Last Samurai*, Warner Home Video (UK), 2003.

125 *The Outsider*, Netflix, 2018.

acceptance.[126] The white male, Peter Kavinsky, is the ideal and the minority female, Lara Jean, is the role obsessed with the ideal—the narrative so commonly reiterated in society.[127] Lucas, the only potential partner and Black male in the film, is quickly deemed gay and not considered a "threat" to Peter Kavinsky's dominance for the rest of the film—the white man's sexual prominence.[128]

According to Deutsche Welle (DW), Germany's international media outlet, an analysis of more than 6,000 Oscar-eligible movies in the United States since 1928 showed that Hollywood often portrayed Asian individuals with racist caricatures, with extremely limited roles, always depicting some form of derogatory stereotype or "yellowfaced" roles played by white actors.[129] It also showed that in the 1960s and '70s, following the 1950s Hays Code era of censorship, came the idea of the "Mighty Whitey and Mellow Yellow" trope.[130] This trope exemplified the stereotypical heterosexual relationship between an advantaged, good-looking white male and a somehow disadvantaged, submissive Asian woman.

Asian men were not placed as romantic partners to Asian women or white women in these films, again perpetuating this emasculated sexuality upon them and removing them from being potential candidates in a romantic relationship

---

126 *To All the Boys I've Loved Before,* Netflix, 2018.

127 Ibid.

128 Ibid.

129 "What Hollywood Movies Do to Perpetuate Racial Stereotypes," *DW News,* accessed May 13, 2020.

130 Ibid.

with a female. According to DW, however, the most common representation of Asians and Asian Americans has been in hue of the "model minority myth."[131] Whether portrayed as educated experts in a technical field, good students, or "successful" individuals, casted Asian men were intellectually or technologically capable beings, with little regard to their sexual identity; Asian men were no longer this so-called "threat" the yellow peril derived them to be, but a concrete image of negligible insignificance.[132]

The effects of these films and societal influence could clearly be seen as a heavy influence in some of the Asian American men I interviewed. For example, during an interview I had with Ito, an everyday Japanese American in his early thirties, he stated as an Asian American guy growing up, one of the most difficult things for him to comprehend was simply "how to be an Asian American" guy. It wasn't that he felt necessarily compared to Eurocentric features all the time. It was that there wasn't any form of representation that made him feel like he could just "be." All the figures that would look like him would play such unappealing, offensive roles that never really gave him clarity on what role he could potentially have in society other than the unattractive, creepy role.

Another interviewee, Choi, a Korean American influencer in his mid-twenties, shared that he often felt insecure about his own body when interacting with women because he felt as if society was already defining it for him. He was afraid he would simply not "be enough" for them. He openly shared

---

131 Ibid.

132 Ibid.

that he would, at times, ask why they wanted to be with him if they could be with more attractive non-Asian men. He equated his unattractiveness to his identity as an Asian American man, which left haunting consequences that he is still trying to overcome to this day.

With a history of not only being emasculated but also rejected, Asian males now live a legacy of appearing less sexually desirable men compared to men of other races. This sentiment is simply the perpetuation of the creepy "Oriental" fantasy white men used to have of Asia—a land full of "exotic" beautiful women without any masculine figures to threaten the white man's sexual dominance. From the way their anatomy is perceived, evident by the continuous depiction of their penises being less than average, to the depiction of their overall masculinity, Asian men have been equated to being "less."[133]

According to a research study by Mok in 1999, the representation of Asian men was seen as lacking in both the physical appearance and the social skills needed to attract a woman.[134] Another study by Cheng in 1996 found that Asian men were least likely to be chosen as containing masculine traits when given the choice of different racial and gender groups.[135] A

133 Murray JN Drummond and Shaun M. Filiault, "The Long and the Short of It: Gay Men's Perceptions of Penis Size," *Gay and Lesbian Issues and Psychology Review* 3, no.2 (2007): 121–129.

134 T. A Mok, "Asian American Dating: Important Factors in Partner Choice. *Cultural Diversity and Ethnic Minority Psychology* 5, (1999): 103–117.

135 C. Cheng, "We Choose Not to Compete: The 'merit' Discourse in the Selection Process, and Asian and Asian American Men and Their

study by Wilkins, Chan, and Kaiser in 2011 also found that Asians were, in general, stereotyped as being more feminine and less masculine.[136] These studies were able to find a multitude of resources pointing to the direction that considered Asian men as feminine beings lacking in masculine traits and overall attractiveness.

This emasculation and rejection is clearly evident in modern dating trends. For example, when the dating platform OkCupid uploaded its data on heterosexual racial dating preferences, the data showed that Asian American men and Black women rated at lower "attractive" rates than their counterparts.[137] Their 2014 statistics of ethnic preferences revealed Asian men to be unattractive (outside Asian women) in heterosexual relationships, standing at 13 percent for Black women, 14 percent for Latina women, and 12 percent for White women.[138] Interracial marriage statistics found similar data. According to the 2015 American Community Survey (ACS), 36 percent of Asian women were in an interracial marriage compared to 21 percent of Asian men.[139] This asymmetry shown through these dating and marriage

---

Masculinity," *Research on Men and Masculinities Series* 9, (1996): 177–200.

136 C. L. Wilkins, J. F. Chan, and C. R. Kaiser, "Racial Stereotypes and Interracial Attraction: Phenotypic Prototypicality and Perceived Attractiveness of Asians," *Cultural Diversity and Ethnic Minority Psychology* 17 no. 4, (2011): 427–431.

137 "Race and Attraction 2009-2014," *OkCupid*, accessed January 12, 2020.

138 Ibid.

139 Gretchen Livingston and Anna Brown, "Intermarriage in the US 50 Years after Loving v. Virginia," *Pew Research Center,* published May 18, 2017.

preferences clearly shows the asymmetry in how Asian men and women are perceived to be "attractive."

"NO FATS, NO FEMMES, NO ASIANS"

"Individuals have amorous and erotic preferences of all sorts and this could include body types, personality types, objects, and so on. Where these become problematic is when personal preferences align with social discourses that reproduce and extend various oppressions.

And it's worth pointing out that the other side of fetishism is rejection—the no fats, trans, femmes, or Asian criteria you see on sex sites. I remember the late Malaysian-born gay Asian activist Siong-huat Chua used to say, "Thank God for rice queens, or else I wouldn't have had any sex at all in the '70s."

—INTERVIEW WITH RICHARD FUNG

As a result of the emasculation and feminization of Asian men throughout history, the stereotyping of Asian men (cis and trans alike) and masculine-presenting nonbinary individuals is often to be feminine individuals, evident in the previously mentioned stereotypes like the "small penis" trope. This sentiment is evident in the LGBTQ+ community, where a "bottom," or the person penetrated during anal sex, is the *expectation* from Asian individuals in the community because of this stereotype.[140]

According to Professor Nguyen from Bryn Mawr College and author of *A View from the Bottom,* it is troubling to find the restricting of "Asian men's sexual desire to that one position" of a bottom because of the sexual stereotypes projected upon an entire ethnicity.[141]

He states this stereotyping of Asian men can be "attributed to a Western colonial mindset that deems 'the Orient' as a mysterious, feminine space to be seduced, conquered, and penetrated."[142] Similarly to how Asian women are stereotyped as hypersexual, submissive beings meant to be overtaken by white sexual imperialism and the dominant white conqueror, queer Asian men are *expected* to be bottoms due to their race and the stereotypes that accompany it under the white gaze.

---

140 Trevor Hoppe, "Circuits of Power, Circuits of Pleasure: Sexual Scripting in Gay Men's Bottom Narratives," *Sexualities* 14, no. 2 (2011): 193–217.

141 Graham Gremore, "Bottom Shame with a Side of 'No Asian': A Message for All You Racist Grindr Users Out There," *Queerty*, July 3, 2016.

142 Ibid.

According to a study by Wilson et al. in 2009, men who used the internet for bareback sex partners often described Black men in distinctly masculine terms like "aggressive," "dominant," "macho," "well-endowed," etc.—words reminiscent of top positions. Asians on the other hand, were labeled with feminine qualities, reminiscent of bottoms, such as "submissive," "effeminate," "small physical stature," etc.[143] Another study by Phua in 2007 found that some Asian gay men intentionally pretended or fulfilled feminine stereotypes to help meet the submissive expectations of partners.[144]

Popular dating platforms like Grindr also reflect this sentiment. Grindr is a dating application specifically for LGBTQ+ men. In a 2015 study by Australian researchers, researchers analyzed 2,177 individuals in Australia through an online survey.[145] The study showed that 96 percent of users on Grindr had experienced viewing at least one profile that showed some form of racial discrimination. More than half of the users recorded experiencing racism themselves.[146] The

143 P. A. Wilson, P. Valera, A. Ventuneac, I. Balan, M. Rowe, and A. Carballo-Die'guez, "Race-Based Sexual Stereotyping and Sexual Partnering among Men Who Use the Internet to Identify Other Men for Bareback Sex." *Journal of Sex Research* 46, (2009): 399–413.

144 V. C. Phua, "Contesting and Maintaining Hegemonic Masculinities: Gay Asian American Men in Mate Selection," *Sex Roles* 57 (September 2007): 909–918.

145 D. Callander, C. Newman, and E. Holt, "Is Sexual Racism Really Racism? Distinguishing Attitudes Toward Sexual Racism and Generic Racism Among Gay and Bisexual Men," *Archives of Sexual Behavior* 44, no.7 (2015): 1991–2000.

146 Ibid.

study emphasized that sexual racism was "a specific form of racial prejudice enacted in the context of sex or romance," a behavior "closely associated with generic racist attitudes."[147] Sexual racism and its prevalence on dating apps, as seen by the ability to apply an ethnicity filter to hide certain users on multiple platforms, promote a problematic normalization of racism.

According to some personal interviews I conducted with Asian men who frequently used dating apps like Grindr, they alerted me of personal experiences when viewing profiles with discriminatory statements like "No fats, no femmes, no Asians." This was a popular mantra used by the platform users to highlight that their sexual desires excluded certain body types, characters, and ethnicities. Others told me they would encounter so-called "Rice Queens," or individuals who exclusively date or hook up with only East Asian individuals.[148] One specific interviewee stated that as an Asian gay man, he felt some individuals simply preferred Asian men because they assumed Asians were easier to dominate due to their stereotyped submissive character.

In another personal interview I conducted with a twenty-two-year-old Asian American male, he disclosed to me his personal experience as an Asian man often assumed to be submissive because of his ethnicity and frame. He disclosed he was "hyper-vigilant about" his "ethnicity when it came to being gay." One of the biggest assumptions people made about him in the gay community was that he was a "bottom"

147 Ibid.
148 Urban Dictionary., s.v. "rice queen," accessed June 6, 2020.

and "submissive" because of his 5'6" height and relatively smaller frame. He addressed this feeling of having to "over-compensate by acting more masculine in order to pass as non-submissive" because he was Asian he felt like he would automatically be assumed to be submissive. He then continued to explain a foul experience he had on Grindr. As users could select a sexual preference option and could list their preference of being a "top, bottom, versatile top, versatile bottom, or no preference at all, he had listed himself as a versatile top. However, later on, he was placed in a situation by a man who forced him into the role of bottom, simply because he was Asian. Despite verbally expressing his unwillingness to partake in sexual activity as a bottom, he was sexually forced against his will and without his consent by the other man to be a bottom.

Due to the prevalence of such discriminatory language and of exclusive preferences that have led to incidents of sexual violence on Grindr, in 2018, Sinakhone Keodara, an Asian American individual, even threatened to sue Grindr with a class action lawsuit because he was disappointed in the exclusionary and discriminatory language the platform allowed.[149] He told NBC News that Grindr "bears some responsibility" from an "ethical standpoint."[150] In response, Grindr launched an initiative in 2018 called "Kindr," an initiative created to intentionally tackle the sexual racism, transphobia,

---

149 Kevin Truong, "Asian American Man Plans Lawsuit to Stop 'Sexual Racism' on Grindr," NBC News, July 13, 2018.

150 Kevin Truong, "After 'Sexual Racism' Accusations, Gay Dating App Grindr Gets 'Kindr," NBC News, September 22, 2018.

and fat-shaming prevalent on the platform.[151] Grindr initiated a zero-tolerance policy for discriminatory and abusive behavior as well as stating that "anyone found bullying, threatening, or defaming another user will be banned."[152]

In summary, the concept of Asian men having "small penises" or being submissive, "effeminate" individuals has real, detrimental consequences. It is reflected in and connected to all communities, again tying back to the idea of intersectionality in race, gender, and sexuality. Through projecting a "dominant" and "submissive" role to certain individuals based on their race and inherently assigning that obedient, submissive role to Asian individuals, white men continue to maintain their role of societal and sexual dominance. White men, against the BIPOC community, continue to hold the pervasive dominating narrative, interlaced by cisgender heteronormative standards, that they are indeed the "dominant, *real* men."

---

151 "Community Guidelines," Kindr Grindr, accessed June 15, 2020.

152 Ibid.

A DIGITAL AGE OF K-POP AND MEDIA REPRESENTATION

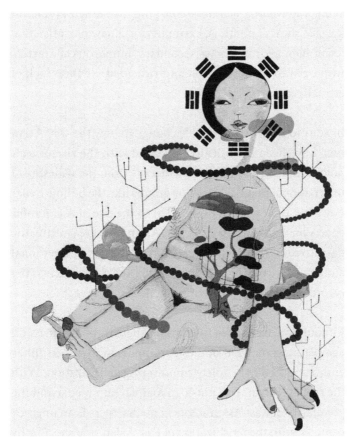

Artwork by Sebin Bok

That said, Asian male representation in mainstream media has been rapidly increasing. From Henry Golding's role in *Crazy Rich Asians* to Simu Liu's casting in *Shang-Chi* and the *Legend of the Ten Rings*, Asian male actors have been playing primary roles that have historically only been available for non-Asian actors.[153],[154] Actors like Justin H. Min, Steven Yeun, and Manny Jacinto are playing instrumental roles in key TV shows and films, exemplifying a new narrative that Asian men are not always secondary, humorous characters who exist to be humiliated and ridiculed for their lack of attractiveness.[155],[156],[157]

In addition, there is a notable change in how the way Asian men have been historically perceived with the rise of technology and social media. Whether it's from the widespread international popularity of boy groups like the billion-dollar boy band the Bangtan Boys (BTS) or the rise of Asian influencers on platforms like TikTok, Asian men are shifting the narrative on their own terms. More than ever, international audiences are tuning into Asian films and shows such as the record-breaking, Oscar-winning movie, *Parasite*.[158]

Although such change is wondrous, there is yet another shift against marginalized bodies coming from what was inherently supposed to be solely empowering: fetishization. With the rise of Korean pop music in mainstream media and the popularity of East Asian actors in media, there is an unprecedented rise in the fetishization of East Asian, and specifically, Korean men.

---

153 "Crazy Rich Asians," IMDb (IMDb.com, August 15, 2018).

154 "Shang-Chi and the Legend of the Ten Rings," IMDb (IMDb.com, July 8, 2021).

155 "Justin H. Min," IMDb (IMDb.com), accessed August 5, 2020.

156 "Steven Yeun," IMDb (IMDb.com), accessed August 5, 2020,

157 "Manny Jacinto," IMDb (IMDb.com), accessed September 5, 2020.

158 *"Parasite.* CJ Entertainment, November 8, 2019.

From obsessive fans who borderline worship their favorite K-POP stars to individuals who participate in "sasaeng" or stalking and invasive "stanning" culture, there has been a rise of fetishizing these male celebrities internationally. This behavior and popularity are said to ripple across different platforms and social media sites. For example, on the popular platform TikTok with more than eight hundred million active users worldwide, there is a trend of East Asian men obtaining fame and popularity for "being or looking Korean."[159] To analyze such a phenomenon, I reached out to Suhan Park and Fred Liu, two Asian influencers with five hundred thousand fans and one million fans on the platform, respectively.

In my interview with Suhan Park, a Korean influencer based in the United States, I learned he had started his TikTok channel to empower his followers' pride for their ethnicity and heritage, something he found relatively rare in BIPOC individuals in the United States. Park noted that he understood the toxicity of the "nerdy" or "effeminate" Asian male stereotype as well as the "shame" many Asian Americans carried with their identity, so he specifically made content to deliberately debunk these painful associations. Park mentioned that he often encountered fans "fetishizing" him for his Korean ethnicity, using it to generalize who he was and was like as a person. He mentioned that such interactions made him highly uncomfortable, making him unsure of how to respond.

---

159 "Global Social Media Overview," DataReportal, last modified July 2020.

Fred Liu, a Chinese American content creator, also reported a very similar sentiment. Fred started making content on the platform because he desired to be an inspirational figure to Asian American teenagers and children. He was aware of the limiting narrative placed upon Asian men and the effects of its harmful narratives. He wanted to show that Asian American men were and could be attractive figures in society. His goal was to change the self-hating nature of at least one Asian American individual who watched his content, wanting to instill a sense of passion and artful aspiration regarding their Asian ethnicity. Unfortunately, like Suhan, Fred saw a high number of "fans," who would compare him to Korean actors and singers, obsessing about how "Korean" he looked despite knowing his Chinese American ethnicity.

The Korean pop industry has had a very controversial response in terms of how empowering or damaging it is. With the industry's obsession with light-skinned, skinny, and "pretty" boys and girls, individuals have often discoursed about whether or not this is a positive destigmatization toward boys wearing makeup and being more stereotypically "feminine," or a harmful step in perpetuating colorism, fat-phobic sentiment, and appearance-based superficial ideals. Others wonder if K-POP truly empowers Asian men of the diaspora to feel represented, or if it is yet another step in perpetuating this idea that Asian men are "effeminate" beings with no room to be seen as anything else.

Amidst this controversy, one thing remains: the obsession with Korean men does not equate to appreciation but instead equates to the fetishization. It is instead, similar to how *yellow fever* appropriates and fetishizes East Asian and Southeast

Asian women, generalizing them to represent the entire population of Asia. The recent rise in fetishizing Korean men destructs the humanity of such figures and deletes the urgency in how imperative it is to represent South Asian and Southeast Asian men in media as well. It is a poison in itself, wrapped around the perpetrator's tongue as yet another "compliment" and piece of "flattery." It is always important to remember: the fetishization of *any* individual is never okay.

THE FAÇADE OF CHANGE

I had a haunting conversation with the aforementioned Richard Fung regarding how he thought Asian representation, and specifically Asian queer representation, has changed within observing the past thirty years of society in his career as an activist.

He stated, "When you talk about representation, the reflex is to turn to milestone figures in popular culture, people like George Takei, Jenny Shimizu, Margaret Cho, Nico Santos, Bowen Yang, Ivory Aquino, Kim Chee, Bai Ling, and Joel Kim Booster. Jameela Jamil has recently come out as queer. There are the pioneering artists such as Pratibha Parmar, Gregg Araki, Paul Pfeifer, Arthur Dong, Ming Ma, Quentin Lee, Midi Onodera, Sunil Gupta, Hanh T. Pham, Paul Wong, Michelle Mohabeer, Michael Shaowanasai, Nguyen Tan Hoang, Ian Rashid, Madeline Lim, and newer filmmakers such as Parvez Sharma, Alice Wu, and Andrew Ahn. We can look at the mainstream hits mostly by straight directors such as Ang Lee's *The Wedding Banquet* and Deepa Mehta's *Fire*. I know I'm forgetting important people."

In any case, it was interesting for him that "for the new yellow peril these individual milestones seem to matter little."

"This is not to underestimate their impact, especially for LGBTQ Asian audiences, but they haven't substantially altered the foundational ass*umptions or the aesthetics of outsiderness and belonging. How could they?*"

In other words, the current state of Asian representation layers on the lack of substantial changes in how Asians are perceived. These individual milestones might perhaps be impressive feats for bringing faces, stories, and characters into a traditionally limited space. However, it seems as if these actions have been unable to alter what Fung called the "foundational assumptions or the aesthetics of outsiderness and belonging."

Author and journalist, Sheridan Prasso, resonated with a similar sentiment during my interview with her. In a conversation about her thoughts on Asian fetishization and its relation to representation, she said, "There are some changes in the representation of Asians in Western film and media in the last decade, including films that have sought to bring an all-Asian cast to US and global audiences (*Crazy Rich Asians*), as well as portray more of the realities of modern life in China in an unexoticized way (*The Farewell.*) The TV series *Killing Eve* is also notable in that one of its lead characters,

Sandra Oh, is not portrayed as 'Asian' but simply a character doing her job.

That said, these are exceptions rather than the overwhelming mainstream. Over and over, we still see representations of Asian women as dressed sexily, in need of rescue, and in stereotypical portrayals of the 'Dragon Lady' or 'Geisha Girl' dichotomy... Just in the past week, in recent news coverage of North Korea, at least one mainstream Washington publication called the potential political successor a 'girl,' in a headline, even though she is a thirty-two-year-old woman. Trump has repeatedly talked about how he 'fell in love,' with North Korea's leader, feminizing him."

"So really there's not much change overall, either in cultural, Hollywood or media portrayals in the West."

In other words, despite the rise of representation of Asian individuals in media, the perception of Asians remains stagnant. To this day, their *aesthetics* and stereotypical characteristics are what is fixated on, their core perceived as outsiders and perpetual foreigners. It is for that very same reason Asian Americans continue to become fetishized and rejected—it is not their humanity seen in these pockets of representation, but an amalgamation of the Western view of the Asian outsider, a perception molded throughout the ills of history. Without deconstructing the historical and racist roots of such problematic perception, the rise in representation *will not* create significant change. It is an internal, rotting problem that needs to be shifted from the inside.

**

Although there is absolutely nothing wrong with being a feminine, asexual, or submissive Asian individual, when society overlooks the various characteristics, sexual tendencies, and identities of individuals due to an overwhelming stereotype that extends across an entire ethnicity, it is imperative to begin to destruct the narrative, built from years of Asian exclusion and anti-Asian xenophobic sentiment.

To fetishize, reject, and emasculate individuals based on their race is to objectify and dehumanize them, transforming them into nothing but objects meant to appease the desires of the user. To deconstruct the stereotypes we have built-in viewing Asian men is to restore the humanity society has stolen from them throughout history; whether that's taking a step back from making another joke about Asian male penises or laughing at the next desexualized and comedic Asian character in a film, becoming more conscious of these microaggressions and what they perpetuate is the next step in humanizing the dehumanized.

The answer is not to fetishize them attempting to "appreciate" them, but to treat every single individual as a unique human being worthy of love and respect.

You don't realize that these words they tell you, that you're beautiful and exotic, pretty because you're "different," is a slow, ghastly well of honey, waiting to trap you in your most vulnerable moments.

You lay there, absorbing what you perceive as sweetness, unable to taste its true bitterness. And then, it's too late.

—ANONYMOUS INTERVIEWEE IN HER LATE TEENS

CHAPTER 5

PROXIMITY TO WHITENESS

———

"Ji-Ji, Bom..no..Boom..Park?" my teacher stuttered, trying to pronounce my name on the roster. He fondled the center-piece of his glasses, uncomfortably shifting in his seat.

Oh, not this again.

I fidgeted the pen between my fingers, nervously shaking quietly. "Present! But... it's pronounced Ki-Bbeum. It means happiness in Korean." I smilingly responded, hoping perhaps *this* teacher would learn how to pronounce my name.

"But I like Ji-Boom. Like BOOM!" he laughed, alongside all of my classmates on my first day of freshman year in geography. My face lit bright pink as I eyed around the classroom, carefully watching my peers chuckle on the side.

"You can just call me Joyce," I choked up. "It'll make both our lives easier," I muttered under my breath.

"Hmm.. Okay, I'll make sure to remember that," he replied, quickly scribbling down something in his clipboard.

I quietly shifted my weight to the edge of my seat, hoping to sink into a nonexistent hole and disappear from this classroom as my teacher continued to call the last few names on his list. My mind began to shuffle, panicking in anxiety as I thought of all the ways this teacher could potentially abuse my name as many had done before.

Perhaps a new nickname? I heard Jaboom, Jabom, Kaboom, and even Gibombom before. Perhaps it was time for baboon or boomer? Or maybe, this one would simply call me by Joyce— that would be ideal. I wouldn't have to deal with name-calling from my teacher on a daily basis.

I was daydreaming in my state of paranoia, when I heard the voice of my teacher annoyingly yell out, "Julianna. Julianna? Earth to Julianna?"

I looked up, wondering why no one was responding to their name.

"Ah, finally she looks up."

I confusedly stared at my teacher.

"My name isn't Julianna, sir." I answered. "It's Joyce."

"Joyce, Julianna, Jazzy—the same thing. You Asians look the same anyway."

"Excuse me?"

He ignored my last remark, turning around to repeat the question I had initially missed. "So, *Joyce*, can you or can you not read this portion of the textbook for us?"

***

Artwork by Youjin Choi

GIBOOM

Growing up, I was called a fair share of names. Some, of course, from the complex phonation that erupts from the Korean language that inevitably led to accidental name-calling. Others, from the countless "nicknames" assigned to me in preference for the speaker's comfort, ignorant of my own sensitivity.

Whether that was to perpetuate a humorous take on what my parents originally deemed a beautiful name or to "simply" call my name, "Giboom" was never pronounced "Giboom."

Naturally, I began to feel a sense of disgust and tingling shame when I was called by the name, "Giboom." Whether that was the horrendously mispronounced anglicized version of "Giboom" or the accurately pronounced "기쁨" that my Korean parents would yell at me for me to come to eat dinner, my body began to jolt a little every time I heard it. I could never put my finger on why it made me uncomfortable, but I understood I felt this strange need to scratch out of my body. It was odd to say the least—I mean, who felt anxiety hearing their own name?

My anxiety surrounding my name eventually got so bad, I decided to add in the anglicized name "Joyce." I was hoping to maintain some form of my Korean name's original meaning of happiness while making my name easier to pronounce for English speakers. I was ecstatic to have finally found an escape from Giboom; Joyce was going to be the answer to my problems—the signifier to a completely new, adjusted identity.

However, despite my desperate wishes of a new life with Joyce, I began to hear the infamous: "All Asians look the same so I'm going to call you the name of the other Asian girl from second period" trope. I was congratulated by my principal for a play I wasn't in, called to the teacher's office for an award I didn't receive, and forgotten by my classmates who couldn't depict my name and another Asian girl's name apart. Despite trying to go by Joyce to avoid the name-calling I encountered with Giboom, I was never called Joyce. I was Katherine, Carol, Jazzy, Jaqueline, Julie, and Julianna—sometimes even Justin.

I was forgotten.

My name, the simplest yet powerful label representing one's identity, was constantly mispronounced and forgotten. So how was I to expect the other parts of my being, much more intricate and complex, to be remembered and seen for the way they were?

***

VISIBILITY

Artwork by Youjin Choi

Little did I realize, my problematic relationship with my own name was the outermost layer to a rotting infestation that would haunt me for years. This sensation and obsession in wanting to be *visible* bled deep into my bones, and I constantly sought the validation and approval of people. No, not just people—white people.

Before I knew it, I was elevating the gaze of white people, seeking to become accepted as "one of them" in an effort to escape from what I felt as my skin color's invisibility. At a certain point, this strange desire encompassed the entirety of my mind without my conscious effort in developing it.

Whiteness was beauty.

Whiteness was attention.

Whiteness was remembrance.

Visibility. Acceptance.

I struggled for years, consciously finding my own body, face, and skin-color ugly because it never reflected the eurocentric standards I saw in society. I felt as if I had developed what Du Bois called, "Double Consciousness," or the internal conflict where one looks at themselves in the eyes of an oppressor in society—in our case: a racist, white society.[160] I was ashamed of my Asian-ness and the elements that accompanied it, so I worked to reject those around me who shared similar values

---

160 "Double Consciousness," Stanford Encyclopedia of Philosophy, first published March 21, 2016.

that I so hated in myself. I found myself seeking the affirmations of my white friends, trying to prove to them that I was not like the "uncool" and "nerdy" Asians—I wanted to be different.

In other words, I didn't want to be Asian.

I cemented in my mind that my role in society was to emphasize my proximity to whiteness. My only route to success and happiness, in the twisted and hurt mind of mine, was to reject all aspects of my actual identity, and to live with the labels I was given by white people—all for the hopes of becoming *seen* by them. I placed myself in a box of what an Asian American was *supposed to be like,* in relation to whiteness.

It wasn't a train of thought I was fully conscious of nor a thought I would explicitly tell people. Instead, I buried it deep in my heart and carried it with me, altering my every thought with its quiet oversight. It was its subtleness that made such prejudice dangerous—I was unaware of how much of a double-edged sword this obsession with whiteness was to my own soul nor to others around me. For every hateful glance of discomfort I perpetuated at my Asian peers, I scratched a mark on my own heart. For every lie I spoke of to keep up this "whiteness" facade, I felt a small glimpse of my identity chip away.

My twisted sense of morality and priority corrupt with insensitivity and years of microaggressions were perhaps the very reasons I was so "immune" to my ignorance. I was worshipping my proximity to whiteness for years, waiting for my white Prince Charming to sweep me off my feet and "rescue" me from my "horrid" Asian culture.

MODEL MINORITY MYTH

This self-destructing conflict that I felt in the core of my soul is, unfortunately, not an uncommon phenomenon in Asian diaspora communities—a phenomenon created by what is called the model minority myth.

The myth of the "model minority" is the popular stereotype that frames Asian Americans as contrastingly successful than other racial groups in their "academic, economic, and cultural domains-successes."[161] It perpetuates the idea that Asian Americans are quiet, successful, and unproblematic people who are law-abiding and apolitical—all in relativity to whiteness and non-Asian BIPOC individuals.[162]

Sociologist William Petersen first coined this trope in 1966 in an article he wrote for *The New York Times Magazine* called "Success Story: Japanese American Style."[163] He emphasized that Japanese Americans could "overcome the discrimination against their group and achieve a measure of success in the United States" through their family structure and emphasis on hard work. Afterward, the media quickly picked up this

---

161 "The Model Minority Myth," *The Practice* 5, no. 1 (2018).

162 Ibid.

163 S. Cheryan, and G.V. Bodenhausen, "Model Minority," In S. M. Caliendo & C. D. McIlwain (Eds), *Routledge Companion to Race & Ethnicity* (New York: Routledge, 2011), 173–176.

stereotype continuing to describe Asian Americans as highly successful, intellectual individuals due to their grounding in "Confucian values, work ethic, centrality of family, and genetic superiority."[164]

The model minority myth is problematic for a variety of reasons. First, it perpetuates heavy anti-non-Asian BIPOC sentiment within the Asian American community. The myth suggests that, as Asian Americans are successful despite the discrimination and oppression they face in the United States, other minority groups must work harder and have a better work ethic to overcome their histories of failure.[165]

Often, the deceiving "success" trope of Asian Americans is paired with other racist ideas of other racial groups, pitting Asian Americans against people of color and creating a hierarchy with Asians at the top, right below white people.[166] Through perpetuating a competitive system with each other's races and hostility between races, the myth forces racial groups to become distracted from the discriminatory and oppressive behavior of society and to constantly seek the white man's gaze.

For example, in a piece by *New York Magazine's* Andrew Sullivan, his argument initially began by exploring why Democrats felt sorry for Hillary Clinton, eventually elaborating on the "success" of Asian Americans compared to other

164 Ibid.

165 Sarah-SoonLing Blackburn, "What Is the Model Minority Myth?" *Teaching Tolerance*, March 21, 2019.

166 Ibid.

minorities.[167] The root of Sullivan's argument lay in the idea that "black failure and Asian success cannot be explained by inequities and racism, and that they are one and the same."[168]

In other words, the model minority myth is a scapegoat in allowing white America to ignore their responsibility and privilege in addressing racism. Similarly to how I equated my self-worth in my proximity to whiteness, the myth emphasizes an Asian's worth in relation to whiteness.

Secondly, the model minority myth promotes the idea that all Asian Americans are a monolithic ethnic group that is economically successful. This idea is due to the fact that following the 1965 Immigration Act, which allowed immigrants with specific backgrounds from non-Western countries to enter the country, a large number of well-educated professionals from Asia immigrated to the United States.[169] This specialized pattern of Asian Americans entering the United States resulted in the media's portrayal of Asian Americans as the model minority.

Many national statistics are said to support this stereotype as well. For example, the 2006 Census data revealed Asian Americans earn a higher income than other ethnicities in

---

167 Andrew Sullivan, "Why Do Democrats Feel Sorry for Hillary Clinton?" *Intelligencer,* April 14, 2017.

168 Ibid.

169 "US. Immigration Since 1965," *History,* last modified June 7, 2019.

their household income.[170] It also showed that Asian Americans attend college at a higher rate than white people.[171]

However, disaggregating the data reveals a different story. For example, "according to the 2000 Census, Cambodians have a per-capita income of $10,215, and over 90 percent of their population does not have a bachelor's degree, significantly lower than the comparable statistics for the US overall ($21,587 per capita income and 76 percent without a bachelor's degree)."[172] Carefully analyzing the pay disparities in the Asian American community shows that "for every dollar the average white man makes in the United States, an Asian-Indian woman makes $1.21 and a Taiwanese woman makes $1.16. A Samoan woman makes $0.62. A Burmese woman makes fifty cents."[173]

Furthermore, Asian Americans make up a disproportionately high percentage of those living in poverty. For example, the 2005 Census data showed that 11 percent of Asian Americans were below the poverty line compared to the 8 percent of whites.[174] They were also significantly less likely to be insured,

---

170 "Statistical Abstract of the United States: 2006," US Census Bureau, November 30, 2005.

171 Ibid.

172 S. Cheryan, and G.V. Bodenhausen, "Model Minority," In S. M. Caliendo & C. D. McIlwain (Eds), *Routledge Companion to Race & Ethnicity* (New York: Routledge, 2011), 173–176.

173 "Economic Justice," National Asian Pacific American Women's Forum, accessed May 16, 2020.

174 S. Cheryan, and G.V. Bodenhausen, "Model Minority," In S. M. Caliendo & C. D. McIlwain (Eds), *Routledge Companion to Race & Ethnicity* (New

with 18 percent of Asian Americans uninsured compared to 11 percent of White people.[175] In fact, one in seven Asian immigrants in the United States today are undocumented and fighting against potential deportation.[176]

Finally, the model minority myth is a proponent of what is considered the "bamboo ceiling." According to Debra Kawahara, PhD, a Professor for the California School of Professional Psychology, the "bamboo ceiling" is used to "describe the specific obstacles and barriers that Asian Americans face in reaching the upper echelons of leadership and management."[177] Journalist Christine Ro writes in a BBC article, "The docility myth flattening Asian women's careers," that there is a persistent belief that Asian American women "will maintain the status quo and can be saddled with extra work without complaining."[178] She also points out that East Asians in North America are more likely to be racially harassed when acting more dominant in their careers. Jennifer L. Berdahl and Ji-A Min from the University of Toronto describe this phenomenon in their research study as a "prescriptive stereotype," or the idea that racial stereotypes are not only

---

York: Routledge, 2011), 173–176.

175 Ibid.

176 Karthick Ramakrishnan and Sono Shah, "One Out of Every 7 Asian Immigrants Is Undocumented," *AAPI Data*, September 8, 2017.

177 Debra Kawahara, "The Bamboo Ceiling: Asian Americans and the Myth of the Model Minority," *Alliant International University*, May 26, 2020.

178 Christine Ro, "The Docility Myth Flattening Asian Women's Careers," *BBC Worklife*, August 16, 2020.

descriptive, but also prescriptive in "reflecting beliefs about how racial groups *should* differ."[179],[180]

To accommodate, Asian women are said to "mold" their behavior to fit the gaze of the dominant groups, inevitably leading to internalized and societal tension. The "bamboo ceiling" is said to cause major career setbacks for Asian individuals, evident by Ro's reference to a study of five Silicon Valley companies that showed that Asian women were *least* likely to be executives relative to their proportion of the workforce.[181] According to this very same report, "The 'Asian effect' is 3.7 times greater than the 'gender effect' as a glass ceiling facto."[182]

In other words, Asians are often told from a very young age that their worth comes from the white gaze and their proximity to such whiteness. Political apathy and silence are encouraged in this twisted narrative, influencing individuals to abstain from partaking in addressing issues of systemic oppression, racism, and leadership roles. Unfortunately, this very pervasive myth that promotes this idea of "docility" perpetuates harmful narratives both inside and against the Asian American community and bleeds directly into Asian fetishization. The model minority myth and the pervasive

179 Ibid.

180 Jennifer L. Berdahl and Ji-A Min, "Prescriptive Stereotypes and Workplace Consequences for East Asia in North America," *Cultural Diversity and Ethnic Minority Psychology* 18, no. 2 (2012): 141–152.

181 Christine Ro, "The Docility Myth Flattening Asian Women's Careers," *BBC Worklife*, August 16, 2020.

182 Ibid.

idea that Asians are apolitical, nonproblematic people who exist to serve the white man's gaze plays a role in the fetishization of Asian women in problematic communities like the alternative right, involuntary celibate, and the misogynistic.

***

WHITE FEVER

To understand how the model minority myth plays into fetishization, we need to first understand the perception of *yellow fever* in such communities. Or, should I say *white fever?*

According to thread r/TheRedPill on Reddit, a community of more than 14.3k individuals who support harshly misogynistic and problematic views, many users argue that *yellow fever* is a hoax used to cover the "real" problem: *white fever.*[183] *White fever* is the idea that white men are the real victims of fetishization in society, with all other forms of minority fetishization and rejection being overdramatized by marginalized communities to cover up the "real" problem of white men being highly targeted and "preferred."

For example, a user in the community once posted, "Asian women exclusively prefer the company of white men over four times more than the reverse. The data empirically shows that *White Fever* is far more prevalent than *Yellow Fever*, despite what the feminist-influenced media says... the life of *Yellow Fever* highlights the nature of the women to stigmatize men.

183 "The Red Pill," Reddit, accessed March 15, 2020.

In this case, it means exaggerating the reality, and then stigmatizing male preferences as some kind of creepy fetish."—u/jagrmeister

Another user stated, "Also, girls go on quite a bit about *yellow fever*, but from my observation, there is very little of that going on. I have noticed way more of the opposite where Asian girls simply throw themselves at any and every white guy they see, and then complain about *yellow fever*."—u/Knasgoth

Although it might initially seem quite ridiculous to understand, it is an argument brought up in most debates and controversial conversations regarding Asian fetishization. For example, in a PBS documentary called "Seeking Asian Female," the film covered a short segment called "Do Asian Women Have *White Fever*?"[184] In the documentary, many East Asian women revealed they think white men are better because they are simply "more confident and better looking."[185] Some Asian women in the documentary also revealed they believe Asian men are "too conservative," in that they bring about too many responsibilities in participating in traditional gender roles.[186]

However, the documentary continued to explain how this phenomenon of "*white fever*" was an example of how "hypergamy," or as Merriam-Webster defines it, "marriage into an

---

184 "Do Asian Women Have White Fever?" Public Broadcasting Service, May 5, 2013.

185 Ibid.

186 Ibid.

equal or higher caste or social group," is a prevalent phenomenon in society.[187] Hypergamy, a term originally coined in the nineteenth-century Indian continent to translate Hindu law books, is used here to describe the tendency for white men to be societally preferred.[188]

As cisgender straight white men naturally hold societal dominance across race and genders, evident by their legacy of white sexual imperialism, white superiority, and heteronormative standards, hypergamy in a white-dominated society is defined by minorities preferring white men, the "superior" class in our racial and gendered social hierarchy. As misogynistic, white-supporting culture is the baseline of our society, it is inevitably encouraged for individuals to develop a strong preference for wanting white men, men who have historically been the "winners" of our society.

The model minority myth thus goes hand-in-hand with the concept of hypergamy, as it emphasizes conflicting minority classes with Asians as the "honorary-whites," all to emphasize the superiority of white people. Asian women are fetishized as the exotic, sexual creatures while emasculating Asian men as the nerdy Kung Fu fighters—all to emphasize the position of white men and their dominance in society. In general, white men receive the highest responses from most, if not all, racial groups, according to dating application statistics. As seen by the Facebook app Are You Interested and its dating statistics, it is evident white men tend to attract the most

---

187 Merriam-Webster, s.v. "Hypergamy (n.)," accessed March 15, 2020.

188 A. M. Shah, *The Structure of Indian Society: Then and Now*, (New Delhi: Routledge India, 2012), 37.

favorable attention, a sentiment that appears to exist in the queer community as well.[189]

Defenders of *white fever* are problematic because it implicates that the fetishization of minorities is equal to what they define as the "fetishization" of white men. This inherently ignores the role white men have in society as a whole and the overall power dynamic that exists between the racial majority and minorities. In addition, it serves as a form of gaslighting, completely undermining the harmful effects minority communities suffer in lieu of fetishization by equating it to the societal dominance white men have.

It is not that white men are so-called "fetishized," as they are not objectified or negatively stereotyped like other races, but they hold the superior narrative of racial, male privilege interlaced with cisgender heteronormative standards.

ALTERNATIVE RIGHT AND INVOLUNTARY CELIBATES
Understanding that white misogynists often tend to victimize themselves despite their societal privilege in mind, it is interesting to see how communities like the alternative right and involuntary celibates persist in fetishizing Asian women.

What are these communities? The alt-right, according to Merriam-Webster, is defined as a "right-wing, primarily online political movement or grouping based in the US whose members reject mainstream conservative politics and

---

189 Kat Chow, "Odds Favor White Men, Asian Women on Dating App," *NPR Code Switch*, November 30, 2013.

espouse extremist beliefs and policies typically centered on ideas of white nationalism."[190] They tend to contain members who support white supremacy, as they often view white homogeneity and nationalism as two peas in a pod.

A *New York Times* piece by journalist Lim called the "Alt-right's Asian Fetish," found and described the correlation of white supremacists and the fetishization of Asian women.[191] From referencing key figures like Andrew Anglin, the founder of the neo-Nazi website *the Daily Stormer* and his video of himself with a Filipina woman he called his "jailbait girlfriend," to right-wing agitator Mike Cernovich, writer John Derbyshire, and alt-right member Kyle Chapman, all of whom are married to women of Asian descent, the article highlighted the existence of *yellow fever* that occurs in the alt-right community.[192]

A similar article by journalist Dexter Thomas for VICE News in 2017 called "A Lot of White Supremacists Seem to Have an Asian Fetish," also pinpointed a similar pattern.[193] Referencing Charleston church shooter Dylann Roof's "great [respect] for the East Asian races" in his manifesto, Ku Klux Klan's David Dukes and how he was "impressed by the Japanese people," and Norwegian mass murderer Anders Breivik who praised the protection of "monoculture" in East

190 Merriam-Webster, s.v. "alt-right (n.)," accessed March 15, 2020.

191 Audrea Lim, "The Alt-Right's Asian Fetish," *The New York Times*, January 6, 2018.

192 Ibid.

193 Dexter Thomas, "A Lot of White Supremacists Seem to Have an Asian Fetish," *Vice News*, September 12, 2017.

Asian countries in his manifesto as examples of how white supremacists view Asians.[194] Although the article was different from Lim's in that it was less of a sexual fetishization of Asian American women and more of a fetishization of Asian culture in general by white supremacists, the article did pinpoint a similar pattern.

The incel community, or the "portmanteau of 'involuntary celibates,'" also has similar sentiments that resonate with the same line of thinking as the Alternative Right community.[195] Incels are the members of an "online subculture who define themselves as unable to find a romantic or sexual partner despite desiring one."[196] These individuals are characterized by their open misogyny and resentment toward women, endorsing racism, and the sense of entitlement to sex. The incel community is known to have always been a problematic community, with Reddit once having a strong group of more than forty thousand individuals dedicated to being "involuntarily celibate" until banned for violating Reddit's policies.[197]

Similarly to the alt-right, *yellow fever* is a topic fondly looked upon by the incel community. In addition to their baseline of misogyny, they commonly find fault in Western ideals of feminism, favoring traditional gender roles while

194 Ibid.

195 Dictionary.com Slang Dictionary, s.v. "incel," accessed March 18, 2020.

196 Martin Herrema, "Incels Documentary Featuring Kent Digital Culture Expert Attracts Wide Media Coverage," *University of Kent News Centre,* July 31, 2019.

197 Olivia Solon, "'Incel': Reddit Bans Misogynist Men's Group Blaming Women for Their Celibacy," *The Guardian,* November 8, 2017.

maintaining a condescending attitude toward women. Their members often combine anti-feminist rhetoric and close-minded stereotyping of "Oriental" Asian women similarly to the alt-right community, to highly idealize Asian women.

Incel Youtuber, BrendioEEE, elaborated on this viewpoint in his video "Why Incels Go after Asian Women."[198] He explained the attraction white incels tend to have toward Asian women and "why your white men incels" are "choosing Asian women over their own women" is because "Asian women are more accepting of traditional gender roles than Western women are. They act more like females and more feminine. They're more girly, especially ones who are native to their Asian countries, such as Japan, Vietnam, Thailand and such."[199]

Additionally, BrendioEEE continued to imply in his video that Asian women were more likely to be virgins due to their "traditionalist conservative culture, such as Buddhism, Shintoism, or various other Eastern religions or philosophies."[200] He argues that because a woman being a virgin is "the biggest determining factor of a happy, stable marriage," their conservative values make them appealing.[201]

---

198 BrendioEEE, "Why Incels Go after Asian Women," uploaded on October 28, 2018, YouTube video.

199 Ibid.

200 Ibid.

201 Ibid.

Artwork by Kayoung Kim

The existence of Asian fetishization occurring within these problematic communities is the intersection of two popular racial myths projected onto the Asian community: the previously mentioned myth that Asian women are submissive, hypersexual beings or exotic, mysterious women, and the model minority myth. Lim, in her article, explains this intersection of myths promotes the ideology that "maintaining white power may require some compromises on white purity."[202]

The compromise? Asian women.

As Sumi Cho, Assistant Professor of Law at the DePaul University College of Law, explains in "Converging Stereotypes in Racialized Sexual Harassment: Where the Model Minority Meets Suzie Wong," the model minority myth of economic success the Asian community is stereotypically assumed to have achieved due to their work and family ethics, is combined with sexual stereotypes to represent Asian women as the ideal "sexual model minority."[203] Cho continues to argue this representation of Asian women as the "sexual model minority" of ideal sex appeal, like the model minority myth, pits Asian women against other minority women who are often stereotyped to be aggressive and demanding as well as against white women portrayed as more independent and pursuant of feminist ideals.[204]

---

202 Audrea Lim, "The Alt-Right's Asian Fetish," *The New York Times*, January 6, 2018.

203 Sumi K. Cho, "Coverging Stereotypes in Racialized Sexual Harassment: Where the Model Minority Meets Suzie Wong," *The Journal of Gender, Race, & Justice* 177, no. 1 (1997-1998).

204 Ibid.

In other words, the alt-right likes the submissive and yet exotic stereotype of Asian women that supports the white supremacist hierarchy. In contrast, the incel community favors the "lesser than men" and "traditional-gender role" stereotype *yellow fever* has projected upon the Asian community. As seen by the incel Youtuber's commentary on how he believes Asian women are "more likely to be virgins" due to their culture and religions, broad assumptions form upon an extremely vast region that encompasses more than East Asia and has modernized into many societies with feminist ideologies and educated, female populations. Despite these societal advances, the highly misogynistic and detrimental Western view of the "traditional" and "Oriental" monolithic view of "Asian" women, which most communities believe is equivalent to East Asian women, continues to be perpetuated and believed as true in these communities.

Artwork by Kayoung Kim

GENDER-BASED VIOLENCE

While the model minority myth and the "submissive" stereo-types facing the Asian American community have created a plethora of negative consequences, it has also created a deafening silence *within* the Asian American community in its relationship with gender-based violence.

According to an Asian Pacific Institute on Gender-Based Violence (APIGBV) study from 2015, 21–55 percent of Asian women in the US reported intimate physical and/or sexual violence in their lifetime, an extremely wide range of factual possibility.[205] Another report from a national survey found that 19.6 percent of Asian or Pacific Islander women experience rape, physical violence, or stalking by an intimate partner in their lifetime.[206] The 2010 National Intimate Partner and Sexual Violence Study also revealed similar findings, with one in five AAPI women reporting experiencing rape, physical violence, or stalking.[207] It is estimated that 20 percent of AAPI women have experienced some form of contact sexual violence, with 10 percent experiencing completed or attempted rape, and 21 percent of women having noncontact unwanted sexual experiences in their lifetime.[208]

---

205 "Statistics on Violence Against API Women," Asian Pacific Institute on Gender-Based Violence, last modified October 1, 2020.

206 M.C. Black et al., "The National Intimate Partner and Sexual Violence Survey (NISVS): 2010-2012 State Report," *Atlanta, GA: National Center for Injury Prevention and Control, Centers for Disease Control and Prevention,* (2017).

207 Ibid.

208 Ibid.

In the National Latino and Asian American Study (NLAAS Study), an analysis of 1,470 NLAAS of Asian descent and married or living with an opposite-sex partner found that 10.2 percent of Asian women reported experiencing "minor violence" (pushing, grabbing, shoving, throwing something, slapping).[209] Another 1.5 percent reported "severe violence" (kicking, biting, hitting with a fist, choking, scalding, burning, and threatening with a knife or gun).[210] A subsample of 543 Asian women from the initial data between eighteen and sixty-five years old of women who had been married for more than five years found that married Asian women whose income was equal to or higher than that of their husband were more likely to report having experienced physical violence by their husband compared to those whose income was lower than their husband.[211] In addition, the probability of a husband's violence against wives was higher when wives had a more significant share of household chores.[212]

Additionally, a study published in the *Californian Journal of Health Promotion* in 2010 found that 35 percent of undergraduate female students experienced some form of sexual assault

---

209 Doris F. Chang, Biing-Jiun Shen, and David Takeuchi, "Prevalence and Demographic Correlates of Intimate Partner Violence in Asian Americans," *International Journal of Law and Psychiatry* 32, no. 3 (2009): 167–175.

210 Ibid.

211 Grace H. Chung, M. Belinda Tucker, David Takeuchi, "Wives' Relative Income Production and Household Male Dominance: Examining Violence among Asian American Enduring Couples," *Family Relations* 57, no. 2 (2008): 227–238.

212 Ibid.

in their lifetime, with 54 percent of them reporting their most recent incident in college.[213] "Chinese, South Asian, and Filipina" women were found to be the ethnic subgroups who reported higher sexual assault prevalence during college than any other ethnic group.[214]

DATA DISAGGREGATION

In other words, gender-based violence is a very real and dominant issue in the Asian American community. However, compared to other ethnic groups, these statistics technically belie on the relatively low side. For example, while 19.6 percent of Asian or Pacific Islander report experiencing rape, physical violence, and/or stalking by an intimate partner in their lifetime, 46 percent of American Indian or Alaska Native women, 43.7 percent of Black women, 37.1 percent of Hispanic women, and 34.6 percent of white women report similar experiences.[215] For this reason, sexual assault and sexual violence against AAPI women are overlooked, promoting this idea that there is no need to focus on the narratives of Asian women. Unfortunately, this results from aggregated data that assumes more than forty different ethnic groups

213 D. P. Sehnoy et al., "Breaking Down the Silence: A Study Examining Patterns of Sexual Assault and Subsequent Disclosure among Ethnic Groups of Asian Pacific Islander College Women," *Californian Journal of Health Promotion* 7, no. 2 (2009): 78–91.

214 Ibid.

215 M.C. Black et al, "The National Intimate Partner and Sexual Violence Survey (NISVS): 2010 Summary Report," *National Center for Injury Prevention and Control, Centers for Disease Control and Prevention*, published November 2011.

to be of a monolithic identity, and the existence of stigma fueled by the previously mentioned model minority myth.

However, disaggregating the data *immediately* portrays a completely different narrative. According to an intimate study of 143 domestic violence survivors, 56 percent of Filipina women and 64 percent of Indian and Pakistani women report having experienced sexual violence.[216] In another study of 211 Japanese immigrant and Japanese American women in the Los Angeles County, 61.1 percent report having experienced some form of physical, emotional, or sexual intimate partner violence that they considered abusive, and 29.9 percent report experiencing sexual violence at the hands of an intimate partner during their lifetime.[217] Another study of 160 South Asian women married or in a heterosexual relationship found that 40.8 percent report experiencing physical or sexual abuse by their current male partners and 36.9 percent report some form of IPV in the past year.[218] Disaggregated data easily shows why this monolithic data aggregation on the Asian American community erases the extent of how problematic gender-based violence in the program is.

---

216 "Lifecourse Experiences of Intimate Partner Violence and Help-Seeking among Filipina, India, and Pakistani Women, 2010," Asian Pacific Institute on Gender-Based Violence, last modified April 22, 2020.

217 Mieko Yoshihama, "Domestic Violence against Women of Japanese Descent in Los Angeles: Two Methods of Estimating Prevalence," *Violence Against Women* 5 (1999): 869–897.

218 Anita Raj and Jay G. Silverman, "Intimate Partner Violence amongst South Asian Women in Greater Boston," *Journal of the American Medical Women's Association* 57, no. 2 (Spring 2002): 111–114.

STIGMA

These lower rates of reporting and the underrepresenting data are due to the reality that it is typically harder for Asian American women to report incidents of gender-based violence due to stigma. This stigma is generally a combination of the Model Minority Myth that emphasizes the nondisruptiveness of the Asian individual and of cultural elements, which typically consider topics of sex taboo, make it even harder for Asian women to report of such cases.

In 2019, two Asian women of high profile revealed their experiences of gender-based violence. One was Rowena Chiu, an individual who accused her former boss, Harvey Weinstein, of attempted rape.[219] Another was Chanel Miller, the survivor who accused Stanford student, Brock Turner, of raping her back in 2015.[220] In 2020, Evelyn Yang, wife of former Democratic presidential candidate, Andrew Yang, revealed that she was sexually assaulted by her gynecologist while pregnant.[221] In all three cases, the women revealed the influence of the model minority myth, and their unwillingness to draw attention to their trauma, were the reasons why they stayed silent for so long.[222]

---

219 Rowena Chiu, "Harvey Weinstein Told Me He Liked Chinese Girls," *The New York Times*, October 5, 2019.

220 Yuliya Talmazan, "Chanel Miller, Woman Sexually Assaulted by Brock Turner, Speaks Out in First Interview," *NBC News*, September 23, 2019.

221 Dana Bash, Bridget Nolan, Nelli Black, and Patricia DiCarlo, "Exclusive: Evelyn Yang Reveals She Was Sexually Assaulted by Her OB-GYN While Pregnant," *CNN Politics*, January 17, 2020.

222 Alexandra Ma, "Asian Women Find It Harder Than Ever to Speak Out about Sexual Assault. Evelyn Yang's Story Is Challenging That," *Insider*,

In Chanel Miller's book, *Know My Name*, she wrote, "I was waiting to be knocked back down to size, to the small place I imagined I belonged. I had grown up in the margins; in the media, Asian Americans were assigned side roles, submissive, soft-spoken secondary characters."[223] Chiu, a British-Chinese, similarly wrote in *The New York Times* in 2019, "The idea of the Asian immigrant 'model minority' is a cliché, but at least in my British-Chinese family, we were afraid of standing out. I was taught not to talk back—to aunties and uncles, to my parents, to my teachers, to perfect strangers. I learned the social benefits of being deferential, polite, and well-behaved. As with many Asian women, this meant that I was visible as a sex object, invisible as a person. Harvey may not have created this imbalance, but he and many others have capitalized on it, knowingly or unknowingly, to abuse women of color."[224]

Similar sentiments were directly represented in interviews I conducted with Asian American women myself. For example, in a qualitative interview I conducted with a twenty-year-old college student, an individual shared her experience of how a seemingly "normal" relationship with her boyfriend quickly warped into traumatic fetishization and, eventually, rape. She was unaware that her boyfriend had any form of "fetish" or racial "preference" at first, as it had felt like any other campus couple relationship—one full of attraction, light-hearted memories, and sexual experiences. Unfortunately,

---

January 18, 2020.

223 Chanel Miller, *Know My Name: A Memoir* (Penguin, 2020), 250.

224 Rowena Chiu, "Harvey Weinstein Told Me He Liked Chinese Girls," *The New York Times*, October 5, 2019.

her relationship became riddled with microaggressions from both her boyfriend and his friends as time passed; she later learned that in the past, he had only dated East Asian women, and when she began to question his motives in meeting her, he angrily lashed back in justification of his preferences. Unfortunately, due to the unequal power dynamic between the two, she felt it would be better to end the relationship than to continue questioning his racist values. Although her respects were kept for the time being, when she later encountered him at a party a few months later, he continued to perpetuate this unequal power dynamic and eventually raped her. Despite this horrendous act of gender-based violence, she chose not to report this incident to the authorities or her family due to its effects on her mental health and overall stigma surrounding the subject.

Another qualitative interview I conducted with a working individual in her twenties resonated with a similar experience. This individual shared that when she had just graduated from high school, she was unknowingly targeted by an online predator because of her Korean ethnicity; a handsome, slightly older white male messaged her through social media and complimented her attractiveness. As he had a strong online presence and following, she believed him to be a harmless individual and was flattered that a famous person was paying her attention. Over time, she gave her trust to him, as he had constantly showered her with compliments and feel-good comments, eventually entering into a romantic relationship with him. Later on, however, he began to emphasize that his attraction to her was solely physical based, pressuring her to send him explicit photos of herself nude. The unequal power dynamic between the two eventually led to him making the individual send him a photo of herself, which he later kept, threatening to release it when she began questioning their relationship. Soon after, when she realized that this man had only targeted her because of her Korean ethnicity and was conducting the same behavior with other Korean women on social media, she decided to cut him off. Unfortunately, for multiple months after, he continued to approach her through different social media platforms, threatening to stalk her at her college campus and to expose her sexts on the internet. Similarly to the other interviewee, she felt unable to report this harassment to those around her and her family because of stigma and the lack of these types of conversations generally being held in the Asian American community.

According to the National Latino and Asian American Study, findings show that among AAPI groups, men are more likely to report perpetrating IPV (Intimate Partner Violence) than women are to report experiencing it, as there are high rates of victimization than perpetration and extreme stigma attached to being a victim.[225] This contrasts most IPV studies that show victims tend to report at higher rates than perpetrators.[226]

---

225 Cathy Hu, "What We Know about Intimate Partner Violence in Asian American and Pacific Islander Communities," *Urban Institute*, May 31, 2018.

226 David B. Sugarman and Gerald T. Hotaling, "Intimate Violence and Social Desirability: A Meta-Analytic Review," *Journal of Interpersonal Violence* 12, no. 2 (1997): 275–290.

In addition, internalized traditional gender norms that per-petuate gender-based violence and misogyny play a signifi-cant role in preventing women from reporting such incidents, as it "influences how gender violence is viewed: minimized by society as an accidental problem."[227] The admittance or reporting of sexual or physical assault would threaten famil-ial shame and "purity" culture that often accompanies such misogynic norms, and disrupts the "model minority" myth that portrays Asian Americans as silent and nonproblematic people.

To better understand the significance of sexual violence in the Asian American community, I reached out to Grace Poon Ghaffari, a Sexual Violence Prevention Specialist at Stanford University's Office of Sexual Assault and Relationship Edu-cation & Response (SARA). She recently started an organiza-tion called Asian Women College Survivors, an organization striving to focus on the intersections of campus sexual vio-lence and women's survivors. She explained she wanted to create a collective community centered on Asian survivors of gender-based violence with the context of higher education, wanting to center on Asian cis and trans women stories.

She explained the sexual assault of women in the AAPI community was extremely prevalent, but even more so underreported. When comparing rates of victimization, Asian women were quantitatively found to have lower rates than other ethnicities due to a combination of stigma, col-lective cultural shame, as well as the overwhelming role of

227 "Culture & Gender-Based Violence," Asian Pacific Institute on Gen-der-Based Violence, last modified September 28, 2020.

the "model minority" myth, thus confirming the correlation between gender-based violence and this myth. Reported narratives are erased, overlooked, and considered "outliers" due to the assumption that low statistics on Asian gender-based violence accurately represent the lack of sexual violence in the community.

Artwork by Claire Cai

The "sexual" model minority myth is extremely dangerous because it imposes this idea that Asian women are sexual objects meant to serve the white male hierarchy while promoting the idea that they are to remain nondisruptive and hardworking beings under the white gaze. They have the difficult dilemma of being fetishized while not having an outlet to report such fetishization and gender-based violence that potentially could be occurring. Similarly to how the misogynists argued for "*white fever*," the narratives of Asian American women are often shadowed by the toxicity and stereotypes surrounding our ethnicity, erased once again by those who maintain a dominant position against us in society.

TIME MACHINE

Looking back, I wish I could whisper into the ears of the ninth-grade girl shaking in her seat as her teacher mispronounced her name that there is no need to work so hard to "feel seen" and "accepted." I wish I could let her know how beautiful her Korean name is, preventing the painful transition into forcibly accepting Joyce in the first place. I wish I could talk to her about her "need" to feel accepted by a white community, and why she didn't need to stay "quiet" and "unproblematic" to the white gaze.

Unfortunately, time cannot turn back, and the scars left from the remnants of these memories will be engrained within me forever. Despite learning how problematic the model minority myth is and acknowledging my elevation of white people occurring from my upbringing, these scars left inside of me will take many more years of active unlearning to fade.

We, as Asian American women, do not exist to sexually appease or to elevate the white man. Our roles in society do not equate to the small box of stereotypes the model minority myth places upon us, silencing our narratives while maintaining a position to sexualize our bodies. We can be leaders, outspoken, and empowering, making our own definitions for our bodies and identities in this brutal world.

"When I was still in high school, there were multiple men who would be in their thirties or forties, paying me to go on dates. They were fixated on the idea that I was not only Asian, but an Asian girl in high school.

***

This one time, one of them propositioned me to do a group sex session with him and his friends because he felt like he couldn't 'miss the opportunity.' In their eyes, it was 'extra points' that I was an underage Asian schoolgirl."

—ANONYMOUS INTERVIEWEE IN HER THIRTIES

CHAPTER 6

DESIRE AND FANTASY

On the morning of November 11, 2000, three Japanese girls waited eagerly at their local bus stop in Spokane, Washington, trying to stay warm in the bitter cold. They were students from a local Japanese school attempting to go downtown, wanting to explore the country they had only stepped foot in around two months ago.

Shivering in the freezing nine-degree weather, they desperately waited for the next bus when a smiling woman in her forties stopped by them in her warm, cozy Subaru. She charmingly offered to give them a ride, using the fact they had just missed their bus as a kind, persuasive argument. The girls, tired of the cold and trusting of the woman, hopped in.

The woman quickly picked up two men that were waiting in near proximity. In the span of seconds, they handcuffed and blindfolded the three students, taking them to a house in Spokane Valley. One of the students was released along the way by the abductors for an unknown reason, while the other two were taken to the basement of a house.

Thus began what Spokane Police Chief Roger Bragdon described at the time as *"one of the most despicable crimes"* he had ever dealt with—an insidious crime that shocked the city.

Repeatedly raped, assaulted, and filmed, over the next seven hours, by Dailey and "Eddie" Ball, two offenders who were respectively a former carpenter who had been investigated but not charged on sexual offenses and a leader in a sado-masochist sex club in the area. The two men threatened these girls if they were to tell anyone what had happened, these "shameful" videotapes would be sent to the fathers of the girls.

The girls were later returned to the entrance of their Muk-ogawa campus. The perpetrators were convinced that these girls would be too ashamed to report what had happened, making them believe what had happened to be the *perfect crime*. They trusted these girls to remain silent, a trust eventually broken when the police received an anonymous tip for what had happened.

Police later arrested the trio, including Vickery, the female driver who was a store clerk that sold pornography and sexual aids, after receiving this anonymous tip online. The assailants revealed they had targeted specifically Japanese women because they believed they would be too ashamed to report it. "Eddie" was reported to be fascinated with Japanese bondage videos, specifically targeting these girls because he believed them to be more submissive and less likely to report their assaults.

The assault left the survivors "horribly traumatized," said Takaoka, the executive vice president of Mukogawa. They were afraid of the idea these videotapes would be delivered to their parents like the assailants had promised, prompting one to even express **"a wish to die."**[228]

SEXUALIZATION IN MATURE MEDIA

This now-almost-forgotten crime that left these survivors traumatized two decades ago, is simply one of many crimes that lay in the intersections of Asian fetishization, sexual violence, and elements of sexualization in media.

The offenders developed this overwhelming fantasy of Japanese women, its core built at the elements they saw in bondage videos, and the perception that these girls could be taken advantage of through manipulating their sense of shame. This *fetish* they had developed from their twisted moral compass became a projection upon innocent girls, disgustingly placing hurt and unwarranted cruelty upon them. Unfortunately, the narrative these criminals so strongly believed to be true of not only Japanese women, but of Asian women as a whole, still holds true in the way Asian women are sexualized in adult media today.

---

228 Patrick-John Garmoe, "Rapists Place Losing Bet on Victims' Silence," *The Courier*, June 4, 2011.

Artwork by Abby Deschenes

One of the most popular forms of adult media that portray this type of fetishization is pornography. One of the most popular fetishes on pornography sites is of Asian women, with a large majority of the videos of them playing passive and submissive eager-to-please roles.

In the web series *They're All So Beautiful*, filmmaker Lum interviews people about *"yellow fever,"* author Sheridan Prasso shares when she was researching for her book, *The Asian Mystique: Dragon Ladies, Geisha Girls & Our Fantasies of the Exotic Orient,* she found of all fetish porn sites, Asian women fetishes exceeded these sites by far.

According to Pornhub's data in 2019, one of the most popular pornography websites in the world, four of the six most searched terms of the year were about Asian pornography.[229] The most searched *term*, in general, was "Japanese," with "hentai," a form of Japanese pornography made in an animation style, a close second. Other popular search terms in the top six search terms included "Korean" and "Asian."[230] The most searched *category* was also Asian-related—Japanese.[231] Additionally, the two most popular search terms on Pornhub Gay were also Asian-related, as they were "Korean" and "Japanese."[232]

Almost all, if not all, famous pornography websites contain separate "Asian" pornography categories. From XVideos, Chaturbate, LiveJasmin, and Xnxx.com, the most popular pornography websites in the United States, "Asian" categories can be found at extremely high demand in every single one of these websites. In addition to the popularity of Asian categories on generic pornography sites, there are hundreds of websites like Real Asian Fuck, Asian Porn Life, and Pro Asian Porn, which simply exist to provide their viewers with only Asian-featuring pornography. Most of them use labels like "Oriental Sex" to once again feed into the fantasies of the "Orient."

In these videos, Asian women are almost always subservient, submissive beings or exotic, mysterious *creatures* in pornography—the one thing they always share? *Hypersexuality.*

---

229 "The 2019 Year in Review," Pornhub Insights, last modified December 11, 2019.

230 Ibid.

231 Ibid.

232 Ibid.

Simply searching "Asian" on pornography websites bring hundreds of titles that sentiment: "Petite Asian takes big cock," "Tight Asian girl orgasming on big white dick," "Small Asian Teen Fucks Stepdad." If not all, most of these titles emphasize the "petite" or "submissive" aspect of Asian women and the dominating, "big" aspect of the partner, perpetuating again this perception of Asian women as infantilized, hypersexual objects meant to pleasure the man.

Research studies reflect a similar disposition. The fetishization of Asian women and the stereotypical racial assumptions that depict them to be passive, sexual *objects* are often portrayed in pornography through **aggression**. A study by Shor and Golriz, Gender, Race, and Aggression in Mainstream Pornography, provided an analysis of 172 popular free internet pornographic videos and found that videos featuring Black women were less likely to depict aggression than those with white women, while videos featuring Asian and Latina women were more likely to depict aggression than Black and white women.[233]

The study also found that aggression was present in three-quarters of the videos containing Asian women, a much higher rate than for any other group of women studied, with videos featuring Asian women being the most likely to include nonconsensual violence.[234] It also found the aggression suffered by Asian females occurred in both Japanese

233 Eran Shor and Golshan Golriz, "Gender, Race, and Aggression in Mainstream Pornography," *Archives of Sexual Behavior* 48, no. 3 (April 2019): 739–751.

234 Ibid.

and Western-produced videos.[235] In short, they concluded that Asian females were most likely victims of aggression in pornography compared to other ethnic groups. Additionally, Asian women in a large majority of the videos were characteristically "passive, submissive, or eager to please, and certainly not more defiant than women from other racial groups."[236]

In other words, Asian female performers were treated more aggressively despite playing roles of submission or passivity.[237] Shor and Golriz write that the lack of resistance in these videos was "perceived as encouragement, and when they do show discomfort or pain, these are likely to be ignored."[238]

Gosset and Byrne's research from 2002 found similar results when they analyzed thirty-one pornographic websites depicting the rape and torture of women. They found that over half of them showed Asian females as the rape victim with one-third of the perpetrators being white men.[239]

PORNOGRAPHY AND ITS VIEWERS
The online pornography industry is estimated to be a multi-billion dollar industry with millions of users accessing

---

235 Ibid.

236 Ibid.

237 Ibid.

238 Ibid.

239 Jennifer Lynn Gossett and Sarah Byrne, "Click Here: A Content Analysis of Internet Rape Sites," *Gender and Society* 16, no. 5 (October 2002): 689–709.

it daily.[240] According to online studies, 12 percent of all internet websites are pornographic, with 25 percent of all online search engine requests relating to sex.[241] Thirty-five percent of all internet downloads are reported to be pornographic, and the average age of exposure to internet porn is estimated to be around eleven years old.[242] Statistics from NCOSE (National Center on Sexual Exploitation) additionally show that 64 percent of young people, aged thirteen to twenty-four, actively seek out pornography.[243] Despite the overwhelming popularity of pornography on the internet, its effects remain controversial to this day. As pornography ranges from professionals filming consensual, enjoyable work to illegal footages of raped minors and individuals, society tends to perceive it as a "gray" matter in society—and of course, in research as well.

Some empirical studies have shown the negative effects pornography has on their consumers. For example, one study revealed that fourteen to nineteen-year-old females who have consumed pornography have a significantly higher likelihood of being victims of sexual harassment or sexual assault.[244] Another study in 2013, published in the *Journal of Communication,* revealed watching porn suggests more sexist attitudes, according to a probability-based sample of young

---

240 "How Big Is Porn?" *Forbes,* May 25, 2001.

241 Megan Hull, "Pornography Facts and Statistics," The Recovery Village, August 4, 2020.

242 Ibid.

243 Ibid.

244 Ibid.

Danish adults and a randomized experimental design.[245] In more recent studies on pornography, researchers have been finding correlations between pornography and one's biology. For example, in a 2014 study at the Max Plank Institute for Human Development in Berlin, researchers found that hours of porn watching were correlated to a decrease in grey matter in regions of the brain related to reward sensitivity.[246] Another study by the University of Cambridge in 2014 found that individuals with compulsive sexual behavior exhibit a form of behavioral addiction similar to drug addiction in the limbic brain circuitry.[247]

On the other hand, researchers have also found pornography to have positive effects. For example, a study by Hald and Malamuth in 2008 surveyed 688 young Danish adults and found respondents from both sexes reported watching hardcore pornography brought benefits to their sex lives, attitudes toward sex, perceptions of members of the opposite sex, and toward life in general.[248] Another study in 2007 by

245 Gert Martin Hald, Neil M. Malamuth, and Theis Lange, "Pornography and Sexist Attitudes Among Heterosexuals," *Journal of Communication* 63, no. 4 (October 2013): 638–660.

246 Simone Kühn and Jürgen Gallinat, "Brain Structure and Functional Connectivity Associated with Pornography Consumption: The Brain on Porn," *JAMA Psychiatry* 71, no. 7 (2014): 827–834.

247 Shane W. Kraus, Valerie Voon, and Marc N. Potenza, "Should Compulsive Sexual Behavior Be Considered an Addiction?" *Addiction* 111, no. 12 (December 2016): 2097–2106.

248 Gert Martin Hald and Neil M. Malamuth, "Self-Perceived Effects of Pornography Consumption," *Archives of Sexual Behavior* 37, no. 4 (September 2008): 614–625.

Kendall, an Economics professor from Clemson University, found that the arrival of the internet and a rise in accessibility to internet pornography correlated to a reduction in rape incidence.[249] Despite its controversy, it is true individuals often watch porn as a way to relieve stress, using it as a fun platform to become more sex-positive; people can channel these fantasies into the videos they are consuming, rather than on the people around them.

---

249 Todd D. Kendall, "Pornography, Rape, and the Internet," *The John E. Walker Department of Economics*, (September 2006).

Artwork by Angel Wang

HARMFUL LINKS

For these conflicting reasons, many argue the effects of pornography are too vague in providing a concrete reason why pornography is problematic—the use of this argument perpetuates the very same racially charged "fetishes" of certain races. But what if I were to say these videos were not all "harmless fantasies" like many like to argue?

Despite the controversial psychological effects of pornography that remain a relative mystery and a constant source of debate, it is extremely evident that the industry is directly tied to the realms of unethically produced pornography and nonconsensually uploaded "revenge" porn—in some cases, even child pornography.

With the amount of adult content on the internet blurring the lines of "fantasy" and sexual violence, it is extremely difficult to assess whether or not certain content is actually manufactured from consenting actors or is actual footage of criminal activity—especially for Asian women, who often portray submissive, objectified, and infantilized sexual objects. There is no way to guarantee whether or not the content is from two consenting adults filming to please the consumer or a reel of a survivor's traumatizing experience that will forever breathe on the ends of the internet.

There have been many cases exemplifying the dangers that occur from this vague, dangerous line. For example, arguments made against large pornography sites like Pornhub for perpetually having videos portraying extremely hardcore and violent pornography; videos later revealed to be actual rape videos illegally uploaded without the survivor's consent.

In 2019, a fifteen-year-old girl went missing in Florida and was found because of multiple videos of her rape uploaded to Pornhub and other pornography sites.[250] In 2020, BBC covered the story of Rose Kalemba, an individual raped as a fourteen-year-old and who later found videos of the attack on pornography websites.[251] It is important to note that these survivors, whose videos were uploaded on pornography sites, were still *minors*.

The reality that these videos were shared online despite their minor status are an example of the exploitation of children for sexual entertainment. Child pornography is the "portrayal of a minor or a person who appears to be a minor in a sexually explicit act by way of videos, photographs, or other computer-generated content."[252] In 2017 alone, the number of child porn cases exceeded one million; in 2019, there were 18.4 million reported cases of child pornography in the world.[253]

Unfortunately, many cases of child pornography distribution and filming are said to start in the Asian region. For example, in India, a pornographic video is said to be captured every

---

250 Ben Feuerherd, "Suspect Arrested after Missing Teen Girl Was Spotted on Pornhub," *New York Post*, October 24, 2019.

251 Megha Mohan, "I Was Raped at 14, and the Video Ended up on a Porn Site," *BBC News*, February 10, 2020.

252 Milind Rajratnam, "Combating Child Pornography in India," *Jurist*, May 14, 2020.

253 "Sexual Predators/Exploitation/Child Pornography," Enough is Enough, last modified September 22, 2020.

forty seconds, with about 38 percent of which linked to child sexual exploitation.[254]

In 2019, 338 individuals across the globe were arrested after participating in a worldwide dark web child porn website called "Welcome To Video," a South Korea-based website that used bitcoin cryptocurrency to sell access to over 250,000 videos depicting child sexual abuse.[255] At least twenty-three underage victims were rescued in the process.[256] Another case was the infamous "Nth Room" in South Korea, where a group of individuals, led by a man named Cho Ju Bin, were blackmailing girls into sharing sexual videos later shared in pay-to-view chatrooms.[257] They exploited more than seventy-four women, including sixteen underage girls into performing forced sex acts for thousands of users paying in cryptocurrency to access such footage.[258]

In other words, as Asian fetishization promotes the infantilization of Asian women and their "docile" and "petite" roles in mature media, there is no absolute way in depicting whether or not these women are playing the roles of children-like adults, or are actually children forced to play such

---

254 Shashank Shekhar, "India Has One of World's Worse Rates of Online Child Pornography Despite Crackdown, Cyber Experts Reveal," *Daily Mail Online,* September 5, 2017.

255 "Officials Arrest 338 Worldwide in Dark Web Child Porn Bust," *Aljazeera,* October 16, 2019.

256 Ibid.

257 "Cho Ju-bin: South Korea Chatroom Sex Abuse Suspect Named after Outcry," *BBC News,* March 25, 2020.

258 Ibid.

roles. As much of the filming and distribution of such content is done in Asian regions, the consumption of such media in the West might be inherently stripping away at the humanity of these victims—oftentimes minors—with every click of a button. With the narrative that Asian women are meek, child-like, and submissive dolls, the likelihood of crime footage glorifying the rape of a nonconsenting Asian woman or child could easily blend into the countless other videos that play into this "fantasy."

THE PRICE OF "REALITY"

Pornography websites are also said to often circulate videos of real individuals participating in sexual activity, selling its appeal on how "real" it seems. Unfortunately, many times these videos are indeed real videos of illegally filmed spycam footage.

South Korea was globally spotlighted in the past for having this "spy-cam epidemic," otherwise known as the widespread use of illegal hidden cameras in motels and other public spaces to illegally record individuals.[259] The footage would either be circulated in online spaces, or sold to directly paying consumers for that exact camera's live-stream.[260] In 2017 alone, the Korean National Police Agency announced more than six thousand crimes related to illegal filming.[261]

---

259 Hansol Park, "South Korea Tackles Hidden Camera Epidemic with Spy Cam Inspection Team," *ABC News*, June 17, 2019.

260 Ibid.

261 Ibid.

Kim Yeo-jin, director of Korea Cyber Sexual Violence Response Center, once told ABC during an interview, "Victims are often left with no power to exercise control over the videos once they circulate online without their consent. Overseas porn websites often refuse to cooperate with South Korean law enforcement. Plus, the anonymity in cyberspace makes the punishment extremely difficult."[262] The privacy of individuals in their most intimate moments is viewed by an endless void of users on the web, all watching for the harmless sake of sexual entertainment.

There is a similar disposition reflected in "revenge porn," or nonconsensually uploaded pornographic content. From celebrity sex tapes to the type of harassment that erupts when a previous lover uploads sexually explicit footage online, distributors have more flexibility than ever to criminally upload such footage with the rise of technology.

In a 2015 survey from the Cyberbullying Research Center, 1,606 respondents from the ages of eighteen to thirty were surveyed to find that 61 percent had taken nude photos or videos of themselves that they shared and 23 percent had been victims of revenge porn.[263] Of the 23 percent, 93 percent reported having extreme emotional distress, while 82 percent reported suffering significant impairment in social, occupational, or other important areas of functioning.[264] Over half of the victims "indicated that they had even considered

---

262 Ibid.

263 Mary Anne Franks, "Drafting an Effective 'Revenge Porn' Law: A Guide for Legislators," *Cyber Rights Initiative*, September 22, 2016.

264 Ibid.

committing suicide."[265] Fifty-five percent of the respondents feared their occupation and professional reputation would be destroyed by revenge porn, while 39 percent reported that it did affect their career life.[266]

I am bringing up these statistics because with aggression and sexual dominance being popular components of Asian pornography, the blurred line between fantasy and crime can be extremely damaging. Through consuming pornography and other forms of adult media that celebrate such crude representation of an Asian woman's body and which normalize the lack of sexual consent in these highly aggressive videos, the lack of certainty on the source material bring me to question whether or not this is truly a staged performance meant for sexual entertainment, or a real-life footage of a crime scene.

Anti-porn activist and sociologist Gail Dines once said, "All pornography uses sex as a vehicle to transmit messages about the legitimacy of racism and sexism. Pornography hides behind the façade of fantasy and harmless fun and delivers reactionary racist stereotypes that would be considered unacceptable were they in any other types of mass-produced media."[267]

I want to argue it is not only these racist stereotypes that are problematic, but the potential reality that large amounts of victims and their traumatic sexual exploitation are being

---

265 Ibid.

266 Ibid.

267 "About," Dr. Gail Dines: Anti-Porn Scholar, Activist, and Speaker, accessed August 20, 2020.

circulated on the web all under the "harmless" label of this "Asian fetish." To what extent do we know these Asian women who are facing aggression, infantilization, and violent sexual dominance in these videos are consensually agreeing to such sex? To what extent do we know if these videos produced are ethical? To what extent can we depict a video as a crime scene of glorifying rape or an actual "harmless fantasy"?

***

SEX TOURISM AND HUMAN TRAFFICKING

In addition to the sexual portrayal of Asian women in adult media, the commodification of Asian women, and the emphasis on their "Oriental" nature is emphasized can be seen in more direct, corporeal forms of exploitation. The same elements of the Asian fetish in pornography can be traced in elements of human trafficking, sex tourism, and mail-order brides. Although not all individuals who participate in sex tourism and trafficking act upon influences of Asian fetishization, as a significant amount of participants are nationals from these regions, it is difficult to ignore the existence of foreign visitors who participate in such acts and their role in perpetuating *yellow fever*.

According to the World Tourism Organization, an agency within the United Nations, sex tourism is defined as "trips organized from within the tourism sector, or from outside this sector but using its structures and networks with the primary purpose of effecting a commercial sexual relationship by the tourist with residents at the destination."[268]

According to the International Labour Organization report, an estimated 3.8 million adults were victims of forced sexual exploitation, and one million children were victims of commercial sexual exploitation in 2016.[269] Seven of every ten exploited victims of sex trafficking were in Asia and the Pacific.[270] In illicit massage parlors in the United States, the vast majority of trafficking victims are from China, and the second-highest group are from South Korea.[271]

A piece by an Indonesian journalist, Alia Marsha, published by VICE titled, "What's the Deal with Men's Rights Activists and Asian Fetishes?" examines this phenomenon through exploring the attraction Western men seem to have with Asian women, arguing this obsession derives from what Western men envision Asian women to be like.[272] For example, the author shares an excerpt: "*In Thailand, it's MUCH easier to find a non-hooker girl who is happy to be your girlfriend than it is back in the West. To give you an idea—if you download Tinder and swipe right until the app doesn't let you anymore, you might get one match in the West if you're*

268 Marina Diotallevi, "WTO Statement on the Prevention of Organized Sex Tourism," *World Tourism Organization*, October, 1995.

269 Internationales Arbeitsamt, "Global Estimates of Modern Slavery," *International Labour Office*, 2017.

270 Ibid.

271 Ibid.

272 Alia Marsha, "What's the Deal with Men's Rights Activists and Asian Fetishes?" *Vice News*, January 9, 2018.

lucky. In Thailand, you'll get an average of ten."[273] The article continues to outline the reality that this behavior is typical in misogynistic communities such as the ones explored in the previous chapter.

This article reveals the reality there are authors such as Mark Zolo, the founder of the travel and sex site Naughty Nomad, and Steven Maple, the self-described "digital nomad," who exploit this idea that foreign women are constantly in await of a white man to help "rescue them" and to sweep them off their feet heroically, selling this misogynistic conception of Asian women as commodities.[274] "It's all 'expertise' that paint entire cities as dens of prostitution and 'insight,'" Marsha writes.[275] This combination of white supremacy and the misogynistic colonialist mentality combines to bring about the idea that Asia, and Asian women, are "untouched by feminism and the ill of the West."[276]

These stereotyped tropes of Asian women bring about extreme consequences in perpetuating the popularity of the sex tourism and sex trafficking industry in Asia. According to the World Health Organization's published report of Sex Work in Asia, market size is difficult to fully assess due to the largely illegal and underground nature of sex work. However, the industry in four Southeast Asian countries (Malaysia, Thailand, Indonesia, and the Philippines) "has been estimated to account for between two percent and four

---

273 Ibid.

274 Ibid.

275 Ibid.

276 Ibid.

percent of Gross Domestic Product."[277] Human trafficking statistics by the United Nations Office on Drugs and Crimes (UNODC) show more than 85 percent of victims trafficked are from within the East Asia and the Pacific region.[278] Of the victims, 51 percent are estimated to be women, and children compromise nearly a third.[279] Estimates of the Japanese sex sector's annual earning, published in 2000, suggests figures between four to ten trillion Yen, or an estimated thirty-eight to ninety-five billion in USD, with the industry accounting for 1–3 percent of the GDP according to the Human Rights Watch.[280]

It is evident that foreigners play a big role in perpetuating such market. According to the World Health Organization report, the Asian sex market has a separate international market catering to foreigners that is "comparatively lucrative for workers because of the ability and willingness of relatively affluent foreigners in less developed Asian countries to pay higher prices per act than most domestic sex consumers."[281]

277 "Sex Work in Asia," World Health Organization Regional Office for the Western Pacific, 2001.

278 "Global Report on Trafficking in Persons 2016," United Nations Office on Drugs and Crime, 2017.

279 Ibid.

280 "Owed Justice: Thai Women Trafficked into Debt Bondage in Japan," Human Rights Watch, September, 2000.

281 "Sex Work in Asia," World Health Organization Regional Office for the Western Pacific, 2001.

Artwork by Giboom Park

Unfortunately, as briefly mentioned above, children share similar statistics. Child sex trafficking is a multibillion-dollar industry, estimated to victimize almost two million children each year.[282] The actual scale, however, of child sex tourism and the exploitation of children is unknown due to the lack of research and resources available to accurately measure the scope of the problem.

The United Nations estimates this industry could be worth approximately twenty billion dollars annually, with the majority of its activity focused in Southeast Asia.[283] With the growth of the internet and long-distance technologies, child sex offenders can communicate anonymously with other child sex offenders, sharing access and producing child pornography as well as engaging in their own sexual interactions with children.

"I've seen video content of a child that's the same age as mine being raped by an American man that was a sex tourist in Cambodia. And this child was so conditioned by her environment that she thought she was engaging in play."— Ashton Kutcher, founder of THORN and former actor, before the United States Foreign Relations Committee[284]

---

282 Muireann O'Briain et al., *Sexual Exploitation of Children and Adolescents in Tourism*, (Bangkok: ECPAT International, 2015), 9.

283 "Combating Child Sex Tourism," *United Nations Human Rights Office of the High Commissioner,* April 10, 2013.

284 "US Actor Ashton Kutcher Urges End to Child Sexual Exploitation," *BBC News,* February 16, 2017.

Despite Southeast Asian countries and their efforts to recognize and attempting to fight against this aggregation of child sex tourism and trafficking in the region, the issue continues to haunt the region to this day. Introducing legislations within these countries have "improving child protection systems and increased prosecutions of child sex offenders, but the problem continues relatively unabated."[285] Reports state the traditional destinations for foreign child sex offenders such as Thailand and the Philippines remain popular, whereas countries such as Cambodia, Vietnam, and Indonesia are increasingly growing in popularity.[286]

Additionally, countries not initially struggling with the exploitation of children like Laos and Myanmar, have also become tourist destinations.[287] With many of these foreign offenders often being Western, white perpetrators traveling to the region solely for the exploitation of these children, one can find the insidious darkness of *yellow fever* once again at play. Research states these foreign offenders "gain access to children via establishment-based prostitution in bars, karaoke venues, beer gardens, massage parlors, and brothels, or by direct or facilitated solicitation of children living and working in public places such as on the streets or at the beach."[288] Child sex tourists are inclined to places where their activities

---

285 Deanna Davy, "Regional Overview: Sexual Exploitation of Children in Southeast Asia," *ECPAT International,* March 12, 2018.

286 Ibid.

287 Ibid.

288 Ibid.

will go unnoticed and their motives hidden, like regions in crisis and where the risks are small.[289]

MAIL-ORDER BRIDES

The same rhetoric of the submissive, exotic Asian woman can also be seen in the mail-order bride industry, where Asian women are one of the most popular "categories" of brides. A mail-order bride is an individual listed on catalogs awaiting selection by another individual for marriage, commonly practiced by Western men seeking foreign brides.

Most mail-order brides are said to come from Southeast Asia, with a large number of them coming from Thailand and the Philippines, as well as from countries in Latin America, Russia, and Ukraine.[290] The male consumers are most often white males, "typically American, Australian, Canadian" or, in general, Western Europeans.[291] The majority of the suitors who pursue mail-order brides are said to be blue-collar men, as blue-collar women finding "better employment prospects, higher wages and opportunities to move up in the world" are causing blue-collar men to have difficulty being seen as an equal partner.[292]

---

289 Ibid.

290 Frank T. McAndrew, "'Mail Order Brides' Still Exist," *Psychology Today*, November 24, 2015.

291 Eddy Meng, "Mail-Order Brides: Gilded Prostitution and the Legal Response," *University of Michigan Journal of Law Reform* 28, (1994).

292 Olga Oksman, "Mail-Order Brides: Old Practice Still Seen as New Chance for a Better Life-for Some," *The Guardian,* January 11, 2016.

A plethora of agencies exist to solely help these individuals find a suitable bride or groom in the mail-order business.[293] According to an analysis published by the Center for Immigration Studies in 1997, approximately ninety agencies were offering around twenty-five thousand mail-order brides looking for husbands at any given time.[294] Approximately 10 percent of the women on mail-order bride websites were successful, with a total of an estimated ten thousand marriages per year, with four thousand of them involving US men.[295]

These agencies play a large role in perpetuating much of the stereotypes accompanying Asian fetishization, as much of their marketing tactic is to portray the brides on the website as "submissive, exotic, and erotic... sex partners who double as domestic servants."[296] For example, in 1991, a *Toronto Star* reporter described a mail-order bride candidate photo:

---

293 Ibid.

294 Robert J. Scholes, "How Many Mail-Order Brides?" *Immigration Review*, no. 28 (Spring 1997): 7–10.

295 Ibid.

296 Eddy Meng, "Mail-Order Brides: Gilded Prostitution and the Legal Response," *University of Michigan Journal of Law Reform* 28, no. 1 (1994): 197–248.

"Seventeen-year-old Armie Abellanosa [a Filipina] is playing coquette for the camera... Her T-shirt is cut short to show off a bit of her tiny waist, a strategic flash of young flesh to entice foreign men."[297]

According to a catalog from 1987 marketing Asian and Pacific Islander women, a portion of it read:

"Congratulations, you have taken the first step toward the discovery of an eternal treasure that will happen when you find your number one Asian lady whose main objective in life is to please her husband... We wouldn't be at all surprised if you entertained thoughts of polygamy."[298]

Jonathon Narducci, the filmmaker responsible for the documentary on mail-order brides, *Love Me*, a documentary overviewing mail-order bride relationships between Western men and Ukrainian women, argued that the bride industry

---

297 Paul Watson, "Mail-Order Bride Firms Flourish in Canada," *TORONTO STAR*, Nov. 9, 1991.

298 Christopher Hanson, "Mail-Order Bride Business Booms in Backlash to US Feminism," *Reuters N. Eur. Service*, Apr. 27, 1987.

heavily relies on both sides, the brides and the seeking men, to function.[299] He stated that many foreign women recruited into this industry are often "led to believe that American men don't drink or ever cheat on their wives," factoring into the "American Dream" facade.[300] American grooms are thus considered popular amongst the mail-order brides, promising this idea of white superiority, American exceptionalism, and economic stability from coming from a global superpower.[301] The men, he recalls, often seek "sex objects" on these websites, looking to find women who can fulfill the desires they are often unable to fulfill with women in their own nation.[302]

---

299 Olga Oksman, "Mail-Order Brides: Old Practice Still Seen as New Chance for a Better Life-for Some," *The Guardian,* January 11, 2016.

300 Ibid.

301 Ibid.

302 Ibid.

Photograph by Jingyuan Tian

OBJECTIFICATION AND MISOGYNY

Although catalogs are much less prevalent in the modern era, as these platforms have shifted online, similar sentiments of fetishization and stereotyping regarding Asian women exist today. Websites provide a specific catalog of women to choose from the ethnicity of the user's liking. For example, the popular AsianLadyOnline platform covers Asian women from the Philippines, Japan, Thailand, Vietnam, India, Indonesia, Pakistan, and Nepal.[303] On its front page, it features pictures of women of mostly East Asian features, their age, name, and ways to contact them using their platform.[304] Online quizzes allow for users to select body types, age preferences, and other specifics that they want in their potential "bride."[305]

---

303 "Never Too Late to Fall in Love," AsianLadyOnline.com, accessed September 2, 2020.

304 Ibid.

305 Ibid.

Photograph by Jingyuan Tian

According to a blog post by *Foreign Brides,* a website specifically targeting individuals interested in "ordering" a mail-order bride, a blog post called "5 Facts You Better Know About Asian Brides" outlined why "Asian beauty enchants

Western men a lot."[306] It states that Asian women are optimal brides because "Femininity is a trend" in Asia that encourages women to be "fashionable, dress and behave in a feminine way" and makes them have "nothing boyish in them, and that's what makes them so attractive."[307] The blog post hauntingly stereotypes that all Asian women "prefer to marry at a young age," using "statistics" to say that 42 percent of all Asian mail-order brides are twenty-one to twenty-five years old.[308] It encourages the users of the website to "Do the research to make your choice!" before selecting a mail-order bride, reflecting the objectifying nature of this practice.[309]

This is simply one of many agencies that solely exist to help commodify an individual's Asian fetish. A simple google search will allow individuals to enter upon tons of "dating" sites that promise these marriages, helping them find the "tempting Oriental beauties" they advertise.

In general, there are numerous websites that help users find ethnic-specific mail-order bride websites and websites that rank these specific dating platforms. For example, *Bright Brides* is a review platform that provides a ranking of mail-order bride websites and also provides insight as to which websites are the most suitable for users.[310] The websites

---

306 "5 Facts You Better Know About Asian Brides," *Foreign Brides,* October 2, 2018.

307 Ibid.

308 Ibid.

309 Ibid.

310 "How to Find the Best Mail Order Bride," *Bright Brides,* accessed September 2, 2020.

they rank act like mail-order bride agencies, setting up men with foreign women from all parts of the world and providing them with special treatment to make the most out of their experience. Similarly to review websites like *Yelp, Bright Brides* has a ranking system that notifies its viewers which dating platforms are the most popular and the pros and cons to each.[311] The top five at the time I was preparing this book being: KissRussianBeauty, AsianLadyOnline, UkraineBrides4you, AsiaMe, and LatinWomenDate. The website also provides articles to help provide men with "insightful advice," providing tips to help boost their successes, such as avoiding "proposing too early" or thinking you are "buying a wife."[312]

In other words, there is an entire **industry** for men to pursue their Asian fetish, inherently "purchasing" their future wives to fit according to their fantasy of what an Asian woman is supposed to be. As if objectification and sexualization were not enough in mainstream media and cultural stereotypes, the mail-order bride industry quite literally commodifies Asian women and their bodies, marketing this fantasy to its most vulgar and exploitative potential.

HUMAN

Asian fetishization has dived deep into the edges of darkness, sinking into the trafficking of both adults and children, sexually abused, and exploited. With the popularity of the Asian fetish on pornography portrayed through aggression and infantilization, the blurred lines between "harmless"

311 Ibid.
312 Ibid.

fantasy and crime are significantly worse. Sex trafficking and sex tourism—which often involve children—remain a detrimental problem to many Asian governments today. Asian individuals, especially Southeast Asians, are still being "sold" on catalogs in the modern twenty-first century, commodified to fit the "buyer" and his "preferences."

With the widespread "sexual popularity" of Asian women, the humanity of these women is often stripped away, forcibly viewed as objects meant to dominate. The overall misogynistic basis of these practices, which celebrate the idea of the white man rescuing the "poor, helpless Asian woman," continues to ripple on throughout different corners of society. This narrative often makes us forget about the very same humanity of individuals who work in the sex industry, and the prejudices they face due to such painful rhetoric.

To obtain more insight from an actual individual involved in the sex industry, I reached out to Official Kendama Babe, an Asian American sex educator, and sex worker.

Official Kendama Babe explained during our interview that she was aware the Asian diaspora community contained a general shaming and taboo-treating nature around the topic of sex and the sex industry. Despite the prevalence of fetishization and the manipulation of sexual narrative placed on Asian women, she felt this rather silencing element of the community deafening.

She explained that as a sex worker and educator, she aspired to help illuminate the prejudices workers in the industry often faced, helping to deconstruct such obstacles that were causing such injustices. She had found so much empowerment within herself during her journey in this industry and wanted to share such reclaiming of her sexuality with others in a safe, ethical, and consensual way.

Like Official Kendama Babe mentioned, it is exactly because there is a general shame and taboo-nature surrounding conversations on sex within the Asian diaspora community, that it is necessary to converse about the sex industry. It is for this very reason we must deconstruct and reclaim this sexualized light Western adult media portrays Asian women in. To promote more ethical consumption and creation of pornography, the destruction of unethical sex trafficking, and the overall problematic nature of fetishization and its intersection with the sex industry, we must reclaim our agency.

The voices of victims in sex trafficking and tourism have far too long been silenced, while the voices of professional, consenting sex workers continue to be judged and shamed—this conflicting dichotomy that exists amidst the white man's fantasy only promotes a demeaning and inimical narrative against Asian women.

They treated my body as if it was a sin. Sexual, exotic, and full of desire, or a disgusting, diseased piece of rejection. Either way, relentlessly wrong.

—ANONYMOUS INTERVIEWEE IN HER EARLY TWENTIES

CHAPTER 7

DISEASE AND SEXUALIZATION

―――

"The Chinese Virus..."

"Get out of our country!"

"A Korean grandfather was badly beaten at a bus stop..."

"...A Texas man was accused earlier today of stabbing an Asian family over the coronavirus."

"An indigenous woman was brutally hurt after being mistaken for a Chinese..."

With the voices of the news anchor tuning in and out of my ears, my eyes began to dry, watching the fluorescent-like radiance of my family's old television screen flicker in and out. I slowly turned my head to watch my parents, quietly watching their micro-moves—attempting to grab a glimpse of their feelings. My head began to numb as notifications continued to ping my phone, texts, and messages flooding my inbox to alert me on yet another coronavirus death, yet another hate crime.

The coronavirus was an unprecedented event in history. At the point my book was nearly published, there were over two hundred thousand deaths in the United States alone, and over seven million deaths worldwide.[313] It was a nonbiased outbreak showing the shortcomings of American exceptionalism, revealing the cycles of systemic racism that continue to rotate within our country in the form of health care, housing, and crime, to name a few. The world quietly watched as a multitude of governments continuously failed to grasp the lifelines of their citizens, watching some leaders even place blame on specific ethnicities and races—one of those leaders, unfortunately, was ours.

313 "United States COVID-19 Cases and Deaths by State," Centers for Disease Control and Prevention, last updated October 10, 2020.

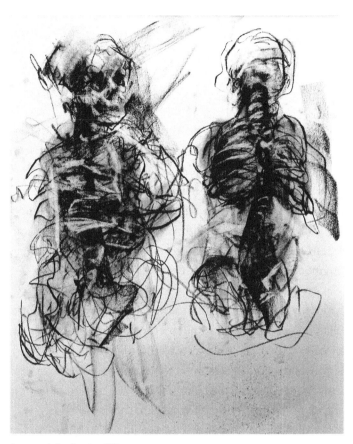

Artwork by Janice Khang

Our very own President Trump called the COVID-19 virus a "Chinese Virus" and the "Kung Flu," subsequently binding the virus to Asians and Asian Americans, with a heavy emphasis on East Asian bodies.[314] I watched as individuals began parroting his language, using his speech as an excuse

314 David Nakamura, "With 'Kung Flu,' Trump Sparks Backlash over Racist Language—and a Rallying Cry for Supporters," *The Washington Post*, June 24, 2020.

to blame Asian bodies as an outlet for their fear. Hundreds of anti-Asian hate crimes spurred across the world as videos of Asian individuals being beaten, dragged, and stabbed stirred the online community.

Only a few weeks back, I had cried at the crowd's standing ovations for *Parasite*. I was nervously sobbing as I watched the stage full of Korean actors, actresses, directors, and staff who had just won the first Asian film to ever win the original screenplay and the first foreign-language film to take home the best picture Oscar. And now, the only "representation" Asians seemed to receive on television and media was synonymous with "virus" and "disease."

For many Asian Americans, the sudden xenophobic rhetoric that flooded our nation came as a shock—I was no exception. I was horrified and viscerally afraid to go outside with my family, scared of what we were to hear by pedestrians or possibly be attacked for the color of our skin. Instead of feeling afraid a life-threatening virus was to infect my body, I was more afraid of the way I was being equated as the virus for my skin color. I watched as Asian Americans like me read how Andrew Yang, the only Asian presidential candidate in history of the United States, struggled with their own Asian American identity. He advised the Asian American community to express and portray their "American-ness" for acceptance in times of more racism. He, as well as many other Asian Americans, problematically felt as if it was their duty—or responsibility, should I say—to prove their worth in society.

Over time, bystanders voices calling Asian Americans "bat-eaters" and "dirty chinks" began to fuse with my memories of microaggressions from my upbringing, teleporting me back into the young, scared child riddled with verbal scars I used to be. Despite being in the body of a woman in her twenties, my mind was back to the little girl secretly eating her lunchbox in the bathroom stalls. In a matter of weeks, Asian Americans had become hated, feared, and violated throughout the United States and the world. So quickly, I saw the world shift its stance, slowly transitioning from fetishizing the bodily aesthetics and stereotyping them as the "model minority," to using it as a sacrificial scapegoat fueled by fear and uncertainty.

FEAR OF VISIBILITY

I was aghast.

I was frightened to leave my house, let alone make eye contact with the neighbors in my small neighborhood; most of them were conservative whites who I could not help but feel hostile—no, afraid—toward. I begged my parents to order food online or to have contactless pick-ups, limiting contact with the outside world as much as possible. There was an "us" and a "them"—a difference I felt could potentially be lethal.

I mean, wouldn't you be afraid if you were constantly listening, watching, and reading about stories of people just like you, getting bludgeoned, stabbed, and even lit on fire—just for *looking* like you? *Sounding* like you?

These weren't legends of days long ago nor events embedded in our history books. They were live stories of our friends, family, and loved ones.

This haunting sentiment of exuberant fear was shared by many Asian Americans. For example, I interviewed Huang, a working Asian American woman in her thirties who had earlier expressed discomfort from the rising hate crimes across the world. She painfully conveyed that it was disheartening to realize that this racism was not newfound for her. "For many of us, we've already felt the bone-chilling depths of racism from the girls who pulled on their eyes in elementary school or the weird up-and-down looks we got from strangers for speaking our language." It was a strange sense of familiarity that seemed to cover itself in painful nostalgia.

I had a brief conversation with a close family friend's son one night, an eight-year-old child named Leung. His father expressed to me that his son stopped *talking* at school to the point his teachers displayed adamant worry. When I asked Leung why he had suddenly become silent, he begrudgingly said, "I know I have an accent, and when I talk, the other kids ask me if I eat bat or if I have the China virus. So, I don't want to talk anymore."

Perhaps the most unsettling experience I personally had with such crude xenophobia was when my own parents and I were on our way to a family event in a hotel. On the way up in the elevator, the two strangers who were on with us asked abruptly, "Are you Chinese?" My father, slightly annoyed at such a question, calmly explained that we were a Korean American family. With that, the two strangers began to smile as they cheeringly stated, "Oh whew! You guys are the good guys."

In the span of microseconds, I felt a splurge of guilty relief, shame, and disgust at this conversation, watching my parents' tense shoulders relax into their resting position once these strangers' statement of nonhostility was released. I hated that I found a sense of relief and perhaps even joy in this brief haven I found in my distinction from their source of xenophobia—a relief that grew into a branching root of guilt. They had no right to depict my body, my ethnicity, and my culture in relation to a pandemic; and yet, my family couldn't help but feed directly into their narrative in an attempt to feel "safe."

In these three examples, the very same xenophobia was depicted in three distinctive methods: in the form of traumatic memories, in the form of childhood ignorance, and in the form of insidious microaggressions under a faux-appreciation. To conclude, hate is expressed in both explicit and implicit matters—in both violence and microaggressions. However, it is reasonable to say that in all of its various forms, xenophobia has detrimental effects on the victim and the community, haunting upon the mental health and wellbeing of individuals.

HAUNTING LABELS

To better understand this topic and the overall effects of anti-Asian sentiment on mental health, I decided to reach out to Jeanie Chang, an Asian American Licensed Marriage and Family Therapist and the Founder of Your Change Provider,

PLLC, a therapeutic practice founded on solutions and cultural confidence in promoting good mental health and wellness. She was a national speaker with expertise in navigating the topic of mental health in Asian American communities and I wanted her insight into the effects of xenophobic rhetoric in the Asian American community on mental health.

Chang gently discussed why the xenophobic rhetoric, and stereotypes in general, were harmful to one's mental health. Briefly put, she stated that this rhetoric was harmful due to its restricting and binding nature. She explained, "Stereotypes are boxes that conflict you. Your identity and what make up your identity are fluid, so the conflicting nature of a stereotype's definition and your identity strain your mental health. Whereas a human being can have multiple changes in their identity and what they define as their identity, stereotypes tend to display an individual as a static, nonchanging being."

She also made the important point this xenophobic hate was often spreading throughout the community by means of microaggressions. Chang argued that microaggressions were harmful in that they were often covert and personal—they could easily make "someone feel as if it only affects that one person it is targeted toward." Although for the average person a news report on a hate crime might feel indifferent, but to a person with years of compiled trauma, it can be quite overwhelming and interpersonal. Like Jeanie mentioned, the personal and convert nature of such emotions often lead to gaslighting and an even bigger hindrance to one's mental health. It was alarming that an often-untraceable phenomenon like this was being massively spread in different forms; from the prevalence of social media and the internet to the second takes and short glances on the street, individuals could be witnessing ghastly emotional costs without anyone else finding them problematic.

The harms of stereotypes, and in xenophobic rhetoric, were apparent in other studies. According to the Bronfenbrenner Center for Translational Research's article on Psychology Today, the American Academy of Pediatrics issued a policy statement describing how racism affects young people explaining that when people of color experience stressful situations like discrimination, it causes "inflammatory reactions in their bodies that can ultimately lead to immediate health problems and in the long run, chronic diseases."[315] Racial disparities in the article were also explained to be connected to infant mortality rates, mental health problems like depression and anxiety, and behavioral issues.[316] Children who observe racism often have depleted self-confidence and eroded mental health, even enough to significantly affect one's developmental and academic achievements.[317]

Another study by Shazeen Suleman, Kent D. Garber, and Lainie Rutkow did an integrative analysis on the strength of current publications on xenophobia, to only confirm xenophobia does indeed have a negative impact on individuals and their communities.[318] They emphasized the importance

315 The Bronfenbrenner Center for Translational Research, "How Racism Affects Youth Health and Well-Being," *Psychology Today*, August 27, 2019.

316 Ibid.

317 Ibid.

318 Shazeen Suleman, Kent D. Garber, and Lainie Rutkow, "Xenophobia as a Determinant of Health: An Integrative Review," *Journal of Public Health*

of policies that "promote cultural integration and understanding" and how imperative these policies are to improve overall community health.[319]

The Hate Crime Project at the University of Sussex in 2018 analyzed the wider impacts of hate crime to find, "whether experienced directly, indirectly, through the media, in person or online" were linked to "increased feelings of vulnerability, anxiety, anger, and sometimes shame."[320] In addition, they found that individuals were likely more "security conscious, avoidant, and more active within the community," with hate crime victims often receiving more "empathy than non-hate crime victims" and often being "blamed more than non-hate victims."[321] They also announced "perceptions of the criminal justice system were generally negative—especially when people had indirect experiences of hate crimes."[322]

The report made a clear indication that individuals themselves did not have to be targeted to be impacted; "simply knowing someone who has been victimized" was enough to trigger these negative effects.[323] In other words, the mere existence of hate crimes, were enough to cause pain to individuals who had not lived through these crimes themselves and to distress the community significantly.

Policy 39, no. 9 (September 2018).

319 Ibid.

320 Jenny Paterson et al., "Final Report," The Sussex Hate Crime Project, January 2018.

321 Ibid.

322 Ibid.

323 Ibid.

BODILY XENOPHOBIA

Artwork by Molly Wu

To learn more about the wider implications of xenophobia and this anti-Asian sentiment I was struggling with, I reached out to Dr. Russell Jeung, a professor of Asian American Studies at San Francisco State University who was a lead expert in studying hate crimes against the AAPI community in response to the pandemic. He had launched a tracking site called Stop AAPI Hate, a website that received over 2,583 documented reports of discrimination from more than forty-five states and Washington DC at the time I was preparing to publish my book.[324]

During my interview with him, he elaborately explained that "racism and racialism" were "inherently connected to bodies," with "diseased" and "sexualized" being words to reinforce bodily differences and to reassert racialized differences and implicit biases. He argued the lash back Asian Americans were receiving in response to the pandemic were simply another way Asian Americans were being objectified and viewed as nothing more than their bodies. The disease was simply another way to perpetuate the "perpetual foreigner" stereotype often placed upon the Asian American community. The disease was used to promote nativist xenophobia by emphasizing the carnal aesthetics of the individual over their humanity. This explained why it was so easy to suddenly shift the narrative from emphasizing the bodily sexual appeal or rejection of the Asian body, to perpetuate this idea that their bodies, in their inherent "Oriental" differentness, were "diseased."

In different stereotypes used to describe Asian Americans, similar sentiments are reflected. For example, in the derogatory slang *yellow fever* itself, the fetishization of Asian women is referred to as some form of illness or disease. It represents something an individual is "infected" with, similarly to the medical definition of *yellow fever*, the "viral infection transmitted by a bite from infected mosquitoes most commonly

---

324 "New Data Examines Political Anti-Chinese Rhetoric and Anti-AAPI Hate," Asian Pacific Policy & Planning Council, June 18, 2020.

found in parts of South America and Africa."[325] Asian bodies are thus once again deemed "impure" and "dirty," circling back to how history often portrayed Asian bodies in relation to solely their "morally corrupting" yellow peril ideals and sexual fantasies.

In other words, the overall fetishization of these Asian American bodies and BIPOC bodies in general, is inherently perpetuating this idea our bodies are impure and dirty—objectified no matter what. With whiteness considered the "default" or the epitome of neutrality, anything associated outside of whiteness is naturally considered unbefitting of its positive associations. This emphasis on whiteness being "pure" reflects on how historically, other BIPOC bodies have been treated and viewed. From Haitian Americans being stigmatized of bringing HIV to the United States and Mexican Americans being blamed for the 2009 swine flu, BIPOC bodies have been intertwined with diseases to perpetuate this idea their bodies are "harmful" to the standard, "healthy" white bodies.[326],[327]

"HISTORY REPEATS ITSELF"
Representative Mark Takano, the Democratic Representative of California, stated, "We as Asian Americans know that in times like these, mass blame and mass guilt gets assigned to

325 "What Is Yellow Fever," WebMD, reviewed on November 2, 2019.

326 Linda G. Marc et al., "HIV among Haitian-Born Persons in the United States, 1985-2007," AIDS 24, no. 13 (August, 2010): 2089–2097.

327 Sonia Scherr and David Holthouse, "Swine Flu Prompts Anti-Mexican Sentiment," Southern Poverty Law Center, August 30, 2009.

a group of people." Representative Judy Chu, another Democrat of California, stated, "They are doing this because they have certain political motives and they are not taking into account the effect of their actions on other huge groups of people, including Asian Americans."[328]

Similarly to how the Chinese Exclusion Act of 1882 and Japanese internment camps of the 1940s perpetuated a "relief" to the xenophobic sentiment of the nation against such "yellow peril" and perpetual foreigner stereotypes, the hatred against Asian Americans is simply yet another way to differentiate Asian bodies while providing some form of scapegoat relief to the erupting chaos from the pandemic.

"Asians caused the virus!"

"Fuck you and your chink ass."

"Go back to whatever shit country you came from."

"Fucking Chinese freak."

"Stop eating bats."

"Get out of our country."

That being said, this should be a large-scale reminder to the AAPI community that in the eyes of many, we are the

---

328 Matt Stevens, "How Asian American Leaders Are Grappling with Xenophobia Amid Coronavirus," *The New York Times,* last modified April 10, 2020.

"yellow peril" and the job-stealers, the harmless nerds, and the "nonthreatening" men with small penises. We are the prostitutes or the sexual dolls—the women in need of "saving" by the "white saviors." We are the easily blamed "perpetual foreigners," the cause of all disease and xenophobic rhetoric that would forever label our Asian features as "outsiders." We are a virus. As if society predetermined the roles of Asian Americans, our bodies and our identities made malleable to form whatever narrative that could benefit whiteness and white homogeneity in our fatally racialized nation at a certain time. And that is not okay.

Perhaps the fears caused by the virus will not be long-lasting, but as author Sheridan Prasso stated in my interview with her, "these misrepresentations of Asians in Western culture have persisted for centuries, and cannot be changed quickly." Anti-Asian sentiment might perhaps dissipate with the end of the pandemic. However, we must not forget the revelation of toxicity exposed in quickly disheveling Asian Americans as the scapegoat of a medical emergency. For too long, Asian Americans have persisted in solidifying their assimilating roles into the silent realms of white supremacy. We have dreamt of being "next" in line with whites, only to have to succumb to a deafening silence that placed us within the bounds of the model minority myth.

On that note, Professor Richard Fung iterated a statement during my interview with him that stuck with me. He stated, "I wonder, what if we take up this resurgence of anti-Asian racism as an opportunity to form bonds of solidarity around anti-blackness, Indigenous dispossession, and justice for refugees and migrants?" Similarly to Frederick Douglass' speech in 1869 advocating for Chinese immigration and writer Jeff Yang's remark that the term "Asian American" in itself was rooted in Black activism, perhaps this anti-Asian racism will serve as a mobilization tool to help us regain our agency in our identities and the urgency to stand for other marginalized groups.

It is time to prioritize cross-racial solidarity and to converse about what our role is as Asian Americans in promoting collective, integral change in society.

CHAPTER 8

CONCLUSION: PANDORA'S BOX

I was at a family friend's one night, invited to eat dinner with their family, when I overheard a chilling conversation on my way to the bathroom.

The three daughters of their household, all girls younger than twelve, were hunched over in a small huddle in their room, somberly discussing what their first week of school was like. It was an odd sight that induced an innate sense of shock within me. The three Korean American girls always seemed so bubbly in front of their parents, but the current atmosphere reeked of meditative gloom.

"I don't want to go to school," Gena, the second of the sisters, sadly stated. "The kids keep asking if I can see because my eyes are so small."

The youngest of the three, now only in third grade, quietly nodded in agreement to her sister's statement.

"Me too. Are my eyes really that small?"

The oldest, Sori, quietly added on to Gena's statement, the peers in her seventh-grade class kept asking her why her features were so odd.

"One of them came up to me and asked me why I had no eyebrows. I couldn't say anything back, so I just stood there!"

In the small opening of vision between the entrance and the door, I watched as Sori grabbed a mirror and burrowed her eyebrows, patting them and brushing them out with her fingers. Gena twiddled her thumbs as she dozed off into the distance, and Jin, the youngest, hugged her bunny plushie tightly.

I started to take a step toward their direction, when I felt myself hesitate before touching the cold, wooden texture of the door. As I watched these girls discuss their fear of returning to school, I felt a strange sense of traumatic nostalgia, nauseated by the remnants of my own memories. The edges of my fingers met with the cold, bumpy texture of the door, intermingling with this sense of unfamiliarity I internally felt. In the small corners of their teary eyes, I saw the aura of myself—the child I used to be—all scared and alone in a world that considered me a stranger.

FAIRY TALES AND HAPPY ENDINGS
The conversation I overheard was a bitter reminder that not every story ends in a happy ending.

No Prince Charming, no happily-ever-after, and no fairy godmothers.

History was already repeating itself in these girls' lives, painting another generation of Asian Americans with the same racism I and many others before me witnessed.

In a perfect world, perhaps I would have ended this book with a happy tale full of rosiness and endless aspirations, exemplifying how fetishization's tale might come to a pleasant end. Or perhaps it would have been a story of the bright side of fetishization, finding some form of light within this choking darkness. I could have written that fetishization and *yellow fever* was a dead and insidious existence of the past, something our generation had understood, acknowledged, and actively fought against—reversing the effects of such an insidious reality.

But fetishization does not have a happy ending because it is an ongoing story—breathing and living among us. It is alive, twisting, and writhing in its void of boundless evil. Evident in the conversation I overheard from these girls and the living, breathing reality of xenophobia and racism that exists in our everyday patterns, the cycles of oppression and the self-hating nature of marginalization were already repeating.

Fetishization, xenophobia, and remnants of a painful history are still intertwined within the layers of our blood and skin, interconnected to the very soul of our society. Its existence marked by the erasure of urgency, taken hostage by the ignorant naiveté of society that continues to silence. And yet, it is completely normalized.

We have normalized its existence in dating apps, hook-up culture, and everyday conversations. We have laughed about the "effeminate" Asian men in Hollywood media, fallen in love with the "exotic" Asian woman, and read articles perpetuating such problematic narratives.

Normalization does not equate to the erasure of a problem—and yet, we treat it as such.

Artwork by Janice Khang

FOREVER-EVER-AFTER

It is a tragedy that our lives are not a magical tale of happy endings of forever-ever-after, as we live in a broken, vicious society—full of oppressive pain and traumatic interlacing hinging upon our racial identities.

However, I dare wonder if it is perhaps the very reason our world is so broken and imperfect that we can envision change and hope. Similarly to how Pandora's Box included the ills of the world but an element of hope that was somehow enough to maintain humanity, it is perhaps that very same element of hope we could apply in this imperfect society to dream of a healthier, humane future.

A hope that can perhaps change the narrative of such misogynistic, patriarchal, sexist, and racist narrative. A hope that can perhaps provide agency to Asian voices; A hope of empathy and validation—a hope of bloody rage.

For far too long, the muted experiences of survivors have been hidden under a rug of normalcy created to perpetuate white supremacy and the gender hierarchy. For far too long, Asian women like me have been painted as sexual dolls, exploited, stereotyped, and assumed to be of a certain way.

To promote any form of change, we must admit to ourselves the severity of Asian fetishization in all of its boundless, insidious "glory."

We need to *allow*, no perhaps *encourage*, ourselves to feel anger, sadness, and disgust—not only for a temporary time—but to constantly allow these negative emotions to writhe within us in admittance of the societal portrayal of "Asian."

We cannot allow our discomfort with the topic to result in our own distancing, leading to a cannibalistic tendency that silences us from within, and that eats us from the inside until we drown in our own blood.

It is *imperative* to stand against the falling tides of fantasies and silence, as for hundreds of years, the humanity of certain races have been stripped under the guise of "harmless" attraction by those in positions of authority—those with the leisure and capacity to prioritize their own ease and fantasy over the actual discomfort of the individuals.

That being said, I am not here to convince you that my personal journey gave me a happy ending full of answers of how to "fix" Asian fetishization and the harms it has caused, not only in my life but also for many individuals over the years. How could there potentially be a happy "fix-all" answer to a pervasive narrative and problem permeating within our society for centuries? How could there be an answer to years of sexual exploitation, white imperialism, and decades of xenophobia that still feed into the way we are perceived today?

There is not.

Instead, I am here to ask of you to simply recognize and understand to what extent fetishization is problematic and stop normalizing this problematic element of society we often overlook and ignore.

It is time to fully accept and deconstruct this rotting facet of society, wrapped in layers of normalization that has seeped into the very depths of our lives.

Change begins from the individual level—from the very personal depths of our soul. If slowly but surely, we begin acknowledging, admitting, and expressing our own pain, with time, it will spread into the community as a cumulation of collective spirit. There will be no limit to the amount of real *change* that could possibly occur.

To begin to dream of such aforementioned *hope,* we need to fight back against such ills painted across our community for far too long. To stop this cycle of hurt that has been repeating itself transgenerationally, embedding within the inner scars of the Asian diaspora. The only way for hope to breathe in this seemingly boundless abyss, is to dream for change while allowing ourselves to vividly express our anger in such horrid reality—a seemingly conflicting truth that I believe will, in its dual nature, somehow fulfill a harmonious future.

DISMANTLING THE CYCLE

Breathing aside my hesitation, I nudged myself to knock on the girls' bedroom.

"Hey guys, mind if I come in?"

After receiving their vocal approval, I stepped into their room and placed myself next to their small huddle, quickly grabbing one of the plushies to cuddle with myself. I fidgeted with the puppy plushie's nose, eyeing the room and watching their small curious faces.

I took a deep breath, watching their tears glistening in their eyes. With an innate push, I said, "Hi loves. I heard you guys had a rough week at school, and I wanted to talk to you about it."

Their faces quickly lit up in a combination of confusion and surprise, overall beaming with a form of glee.

"I... I just wanted to tell you something I wish someone told me when I was your age," I stated, as an immense pressure built up my chest.

"Something I think might help."

"No matter what, don't let anyone convince you, you are not enough. Whether that's because you are a girl or because you are Asian American. Your eyes are not too small. Your eyebrows? Just enough. You are beautiful. It is perfectly okay to be Asian American. No, not okay. Absolutely phenomenal to be Asian American—and a girl? Even better."

"All your life, people are going to tell you you're not good enough. They're going to tell you you should behave or look a certain way to be loved. Movies and TV shows will tell you you can only behave or look a certain way to be accepted by society. You might even run into individuals who will tell you they love you for your ethnicity. Only for your race."

"That's what they told me."

"You don't need to look a certain way, act a certain way, or love a certain type of person to be *accepted*. You are enough for who you are."

"I'm not going to pretend like it doesn't hurt—I know it hurts. Those words they throw at you and which stick onto you—I know they hurt."

"But remember, you are beautiful for who you. Not for your ethnicity or your relationship to others. Not because anyone tells you you are. Don't play into a part society creates for you or feel as if you need to be a certain way to be loved and accepted. I know a lot of what I'm saying doesn't make sense right now, but I will be with you every step of the way to help you and to listen to you."

"You are not their object, their doll, or their magical dream."

"You are not their yellow fantasy."

APPENDIX

———

CHAPTER 1

Asian Pacific Institute on Gender-Based Violence. "Census Data & API Identities." Accessed March 8, 2020. https://www.api-gbv. org/resources/census-data-api-identities/.

Capcom. "Street Fighter Champion Edition: Chun-Li." Accessed February 14, 2020. https://streetfighter.com/characters/chun-li/.

Genius. "Asian Girlz Lyrics: Day above Ground." Accessed February 12, 2020. https://genius.com/Day-above-ground-asian-girlz-lyrics#note-2063962.

Kim, Bitna. "Asian Female and Caucasian Male Couples: Exploring the Attraction." *Pastoral Psychology* 60, no. 2 (2010): 233–44. https://doi.org/10.1007/s11089-010-0312-9.

Lederer, Norman. "Charles Herbert Stember. Sexual Racism: The Emotional Barrier to an Integrated Society. Pp. Xviii, 234. New York: Elsevier, 1976. $13.50 - Norman Lederer, 1978."

SAGE Journals 439, no. 1 (September 1978):193–194. https://doi.
org/10.1177/000271627843900160.

Lu, Chin. "Why Yellow Fever Is Different Than 'Having a Type'",
The Bold Italic Editors. June 3, 2013.https://thebolditalic.com/
why-yellow-fever-is-different-than-having-a-type-the-bold-
italic-san-francisco-36ed29359dfb

Mukkamala, S., & K. L. Suyemoto. "Racialized Sexism/Sexualized
Racism: A Multimethod Study of Intersectional Experiences
of Discrimination for Asian American Women." *Asian American Journal of Psychology 9, no.* 1 (2018): 32–46. https://doi.
org/10.1037/aap0000104.

Schumer, Amy. Amy Schumer: Mostly Sex Stuff. August 18, 2012.
Comedy special. https://www.imdb.com/title/tt2346046/.

Yandura, Kelsey. "Racial Dating Preferences: Racist Excuses or
Inherent Desires?" *Rewire.* February 25, 2020. https://www.
rewire.org/racial-dating-preferences/.

Yung, Judy. "Bound Feet: Nineteenth Century." Chapter. In
*Unbound Voices: A Documentary History of Chinese Women
in San Francisco.* Berkeley, CA: University of California Press,
1999.

Zheng, Robin. "Why Yellow Fever Isn't Flattering: A Case against
Racial Fetishes." *Journal of the American Philosophical Association 2, no.* 3 (2016): 400–419. https://doi.org/10.1017/apa.2016.25.

CHAPTER 2

The African American Policy Forum. "Chinese Exclusion Act." Accessed April 29, 2020. https://aapf.org/chinese-exclusion-act.

"Asian Immigration: The 'Yellow Peril'." *Race in the United States, 1880-1949 Exhibit: Student Digital Gallery at BGSU.* Accessed April 29, 2020. https://digitalgallery.bgsu.edu/student/exhibits/show/race-in-us/Asian Americans/asian-immigration-and-the--yel.

Associated Press. "US Troops Used Japanese Brothels after WWII." *Asia-Pacific NBC News,* April 27, 2007. http://www.nbcnews.com/id/18355292/ns/world_news-asia_pacific/t/us-troops-used-japanese-brothels-after-wwii/#.X3K8R5NKjeo.

Barry, Dan and Jeffrey E. Singer. "The Case of Jane Doe Ponytail." The New York Times, October 16, 2018. https://www.nytimes.com/interactive/2018/10/11/nyregion/sex-workers-massage-parlor.html.

Brodeur, Abel, Warn N. Lekfuangfu, and Yanos Zylberberg. "War, Migration and the Origins of the Thai Sex Industry." *University of Ottawa,* no.1 (Spring 2017): 1–57.

Burns, Iain. "British Man Is Arrested for 'Kicking His Thai Wife to Death When She Refused to Have Sex with Him." *Daily Mail,* April 16, 2018. https://www.dailymail.co.uk/news/article-5621059/British-man-arrested-kicking-Thai-wife-death-refused-sex-him.html.

Chang, Iris. *The Chinese in America: A Narrative History.* New York: Penguin Press, 2003.

Chinatown San Francisco. "Anti-Prostitution Act: Chapter CCXXX." Accessed May 25, 2020. http://www.sanfrancisco-chinatown.com/history/1870antiprostitutionact.html.

Clark, Audrey Wu. "Disturbing Stereotypes: Fu Man/ Chan and Dragon Lady Blossoms." *Asian American Literature: Discourse and Pedagogies* 3, (2012): 99–118. https://scholarworks.sjsu.edu/cgi/viewcontent.cgi?article=1029&context=aaldp.

Department of State Office of the Historian. "The Philippine American War, 1899-1902." Accessed June 10, 2020. https://history.state.gov/milestones/1899-1913/war.

Hall, Allan. "German Man Admits Killing His Filipino Wife and Slicing Her Body into Eight Pieces So He Could Go on a Sex Holiday to Thailand." *Daily Mail,* October 26, 2016. https://www.dailymail.co.uk/news/article-3873742/German-man-admits-killing-Filipino-wife-slicing-body-eight-pieces-sex-holiday-Thailand.html.

History, Art, & Archives United States House of Representatives. "The Philippines, 1989-1946." Accessed June 10, 2020. https://history.house.gov/Exhibitions-and-Publications/APA/Historical-Essays/Exclusion-and-Empire/The-Philippines/.

History. "Gentlemen's Agreement." Last modified August 21, 2018. https://www.history.com/topics/immigration/gentlemens-agreement.

Kim, Bitna. "Asian Female and Caucasian Male Couples: Exploring the Attraction." *Pastoral Psychology* 60, no. 2 (2010): 233–44. https://doi.org/10.1007/s11089-010-0312-9.

Kipling, Rudyard. "The White Man's Burden." February 12, 1899.

Lo, Shauna. "Chinese Women Entering New England: Chinese Exclusion Act Case Files, Boston, 1911-1925." *The New England Quarterly*, no. 3 (2008): 383–409. https://www.jstor.org/stable/20474653?seq=1.

Loti, Pierre. "Madame Chrysanthème." 1887.

Lu, Diana. "Yang Song and the Long History of Targeting Asian American Sex Workers." *Hyphen Magazine*, August 28, 2019. https://hyphenmagazine.com/blog/2019/08/yang-song-and-long-history-targeting-Asian American-sex-workers.

Marion, Frances. *Toll of the Sea*. United States: Metro Pictures, 1922.

Merriam-Webster.com Dictionary. s.v. "miscegenation." Accessed September 28, 2020, https://www.merriam-webster.com/dictionary/miscegenation.

Min, Pyong Gap. *Asian Americans: Contemporary Trends and Issues*. Red Thousand Oaks: Pine Forge Press, 2006.

Mukkamala, S., and K. L. Suyemoto. "Racialized Sexism/Sexualized Racism: A Multimethod Study of Intersectional Experiences of Discrimination for Asian American Women." *Asian American Journal of Psychology 9, no.* 1 (2018): 32–46. https://doi.org/10.1037/aap0000104.

Ngai, Quang. "Unidentified Vietnamese Women and Children in My Lai." *Vintage Everyday*. March 16, 2018. https://www.vintag.es/2018/03/ron-haeberle-my-lai-photos.html.

Oh, Younho. "Korean Picture Brides in Hawaii: Historical and Literary Narratives." *Journal of Literature and Art Studies,* no. 12 (2017): 1632–1644. http://doi.org/10.17265/2159-5836/2017.12.016.

Ouyyanont, Porphant. "The Vietnam War and Tourism in Bangkok's Development, 1960-70." *Southeast Asian Studies* 39, no. 2 (January 2001): 1–33.

Puccini, Giacomo "Madam Butterfly." February 17, 1904.

Ren, Yuan "'Yellow Fever' Fetish: Why Do So Many White Men Want to Date a Chinese Woman?" *The Telegraph*, July 1, 2014. https://www.telegraph.co.uk/women/womens-life/10935508/ Yellow-fever-fetish-Why-do-so-many-white-men-want-to-date-a-Chinese-woman.html.

Santos, Aida F. *Gathering the Dust: The Base Issue in the Philippines.* New York: The New Press, 1992.

Schönberg, Claude-Michel, and Alain Boublil. "Miss Saigon." 1989.

Talmadge, Eric. "GIs Frequented Japans' 'Comfort Women.'" *The Washington Post,* April 25, 2007. https://www.washingtonpost.com/wp-dyn/content/article/2007/04/25/AR2007042501801.html.

Talmadge, Eric. "US Troops Used Japan Brothels after WWII." The Seattle Times, April 26, 2007. https://www.seattletimes.com/nation-world/us-troops-used-japan-brothels-after-wwii/.

Tanaka, Yuki and Toshiyuki Tanaka. *Japan's Comfort Women: Sexual Slavery and Prostitution During World War II and the US Occupation.* London: Psychology Press, 2002.

Tucker, Spencer C. *The Encyclopedia of the Spanish American and Philippine American Wars: A Political, Social, and Military History.* Santa Barbara: ABC-CLIO, 2009.

Tucker, William H. "The Ideology of Racism: Misusing Science to Justify Racial Discrimination." *United Nations Chronicle,* Accessed April 29, 2020. https://www.un.org/en/chronicle/article/ideology-racism-misusing-science-justify-racial-discrimination.

US Congress. "The Page Act of 1875 (Immigration Act)." 43rd Cong, sess. 2. Approved March 3rd, 1875.

US Congress. *United States Congressional Serial Se Vol. 5864.* Washington, DC: US Government Printing Office, *1911.* https://loveman.sdsu.edu/docs/1875Immigration%20Act.pdf.

Vine, David. "My Body Was Not Mine, but the US Military's." *Politico,* November 3, 2015. https://www.politico.eu/article/my-body-was-not-mine-but-the-u-s-militarys/.

Vine, David. Base Nation: How US Military *Bases Abroad Harm America and the World.* New York City: Henry Holt and Company, 2015.

Woan, Sunny. "White Sexual Imperialism: A Theory of Asian Feminist Jurisprudence." *Wash. & Lee Journal of Civil Rights*

& *Social Justice* 14, no. 2 (2008): 275–301. https://scholarlycommons.law.wlu.edu/crsj/vol14/iss2/5.

CHAPTER 3

"Amy Schumer Makes Offensive, Arguably Racist Comment about Asian Men." The Howard Stern Show. Uploaded on March 12, 2017. YouTube video. 0:00:58. https://www.youtube.com/watch?v=x5GJYmW6GN0.

"Asian Men Have Small Penises-Asian Small Dick Jokes-Stand up Comedy!" Comic Comedy. Uploaded on April 15, 2013. YouTube video. 0:00:03. https://www.youtube.com/watch?v=pYn-3KodIYSQ.

Branham, Matt. "Which Country Has the Biggest Dicks in the World?" *Mandatory*, February 26, 2015. https://www.mandatory.com/living/1057233-which-country-has-the-biggest-dicks-in-the-world.

Breakfast at Tiffany's, United States: Paramount Pictures, 1961.

Callander, Denton, Christy E. Newman, and Martin Holt. "Is Sexual Racism Really Racism? Distinguishing Attitudes toward Sexual Racism and Generic Racism among Gay and Bisexual Men," *Archives of Sexual Behavior* 44, no.7 (2015): 1991–2000. https://doi.org/10.1007/s10508-015-0487-3.

Chan, Sucheng. *Entry Denied: Exclusion and the Chinese Community in America 1882-1943*. Philadelphia: Temple University Press, 1990.

Charlie Chan's Secret, United States: 20th Century Fox Studios, 1936.

Cheng, C. "We choose not to compete: The "merit" discourse in the selection process, and Asian and Asian American men and their masculinity." In C. Cheng (Ed.), *Research on Men and Masculinities Series* 9, (1996): 177–200.

Cheryan, S., and G. V. Bodenhausen. "Model minority." In S. M. Caliendo & C. D. McIlwain (Eds), *Routledge Companion to Race & Ethnicity*. New York: Routledge, 2011:173–176.

Chinese Burn. BBC, November 27, 2017.

Chu, Jon M., Kevin Kwan, and Brian Tyler. *Crazy Rich Asians*. Warner Bros, 2019.

Connell, Raewyn W. *Gender and Power: Society, the Person, and Sexual Politics*. Redwood City: Stanford University Press, 1987.

Coolidge, Mary R. *Chinese Immigration* (1909). New York: Holt & Company, 1909.

DataReportal. "Global Social Media Overview." Last modified July 2020. https://datareportal.com/social-media-users?rq=tiktok.

Dexter. Showtime, October 1, 2006.

Drummond, Murray JN, and Shaun M. Filiault. "The long and the short of it: Gay men's perceptions of penis size." Gay and lesbian issues and psychology review 3.2 (2007): 121–129.

Encyclopedia Britannica Online. s.v. "Magnuson Act." Accessed on March 24, 2020. https://www.britannica.com/topic/Magnuson-Act.

Fung, Richard. "Looking for My Penis: The Eroticized Asian in Gay Video Porn." (1991). http://www.richardfung.ca/index.php?/articles/looking-for-my-penis-1991/.

Gremore, Graham. "Bottom Shame with a Side of 'No Asian': A Message for All You Racist Grindr Users Out There." *Queerty**. July 3, 2016. https://www.queerty.com/bottom-shame-side-no-asian-message-racist-grindr-users-20160703.

Hanstock, Bill. "Jason Whitlock 'Congratulates' Jeremy Lin with Racist Tweet." *SB Nation Bay Area*, last modified February 11, 2012. https://bayarea.sbnation.com/2012/2/11/2791353/jason-whitlock-racist-tweet-jeremy-lin.

History.com. "Chinese Exclusion Act." Last modified August 24, 2018. https://www.history.com/topics/immigration/chinese-exclusion-act-1882.

Ho, Bong Joon. *Parasite*. CJ Entertainment, November 8, 2019.

Hoppe, Trevor. "Circuits of Power, Circuits of Pleasure: Sexual Scripting in Gay Men's Bottom Narratives." *Sexualities* 14, no. 2 (2011): 193–217. https://doi.org/10.1177/1363460711399033.

Huang, Eddie. "Hey, Steve Harvey, Who Says I Might Not Steal Your Girl?" *The New York Times,* January 14, 2017. https://www.nytimes.com/2017/01/14/opinion/sunday/hey-steve-harvey-who-says-i-might-not-steal-your-girl.html.

Hughes, John. 1984. *Sixteen Candles.*

IMDb. "Justin H. Min." Accessed August 5, 2020. https://www.imdb.com/name/nm5093708/.

IMDb. "Manny Jacinto." Accessed September 5. 2020. https://www.imdb.com/name/nm3254274/.

IMDb. "Steven Yeun." Accessed August 5, 2020. https://www.imdb.com/name/nm3081796/.

Immigration History. "Cable Act of 1922." Accessed on March 26, 2020. https://immigrationhistory.org/item/cable-act/.

Immigration History. "Naturalization Act of 1870." Accessed August 21, 2020. https://immigrationhistory.org/item/naturalization-act-of-1870/.

Kindr Grindr. "Community Guidelines." Accessed June 15, 2020. https://www.kindr.grindr.com/community-guidelines.

Livingston, Gretchen and Anna Brown. "Intermarriage in the US 50 Years after Loving v. Virginia," *Pew Research Center.* Published May 18, 2017. https://www.pewsocialtrends.org/wp-content/uploads/sites/3/2017/05/Intermarriage-May-2017-Full-Report.pdf.

Lynn, Richard. "Rushton's R–K Life History Theory of Race Differences in Penis Length and Circumference Examined in 113 Populations." *Personality and Individual Differences* 55, no. 3 (July 2013): 261–266. http://dx.doi.org/10.1016/j.paid.2012.02.016.

McGreal, Scott. "The Pseudoscience of Race Differences in Penis Size." *Psychology Today*, October 16, 2012. https://www.psychologytoday.com/us/blog/unique-everybody-else/201210/the-pseudoscience-race-differences-in-penis-size.

Mok, T. A. "Asian American Dating: Important Factors in Partner

Choice." *Cultural Diversity and Ethnic Minority Psychology* 5, (1999) 103–117.

OkCupid. "Race and Attraction 2009-2014." Accessed January 12, 2020. https://theblog.okcupid.com/race-and-attraction-2009-2014-107dcbb4f060.

Park, Michael. "Asian American Masculinity Eclipsed: A Legal and Historical Perspective of Emasculation through US Immigration Practices." *The Modern American* 8, no. 1 (2013): 5–17. https://digitalcommons.wcl.american.edu/cgi/viewcontent.cgi?article=1164&context=tma.

Phillips, Todd, Dan Goldberg, Craig Mazin, and Scot Armstrong. *The Hangover Part II*. United States: Warner Bros., 2011.

Phua, V. C. "Contesting and Maintaining Hegemonic Masculinities: Gay Asian American Men in Mate Selection." *Sex Roles* 57, (September 2007): 909–918. https://doi.org/10.1007/s11199-007-9318-x.

Rushton, J. Philippe., & Anthony F. Bogaert. "Race Differences in Sexual Behavior: Testing an Evolutionary Hypothesis." *Journal of Research in Personality* 21, no. 4 (December 1987): 529-551. https://doi.org/10.1016/0092-6566(87)90038-9.

"Shang-Chi and the Legend of the Ten Rings." Marvel Studios, July 8, 2021.

Smithsonian Asian Pacific American Center. "In Re Ah Yup Rules Chinese Ineligible for Naturalized Citizenship on April 29, 1878." Last modified April 8, 2010. http://smithsonianapa.org/now/this-month-in-history-in-re-ah-yup-rules-chinese-ineligible-for-naturalized-citizenship-on-april-29-1878/.

Takaki, Ronald. *Strangers from a Different Shore: A History of Asian Americans*. New York City: Little, Brown and Company, 1989.

The Face of Fu Manchu, Hallam Production, 1965.

The Last Samurai, Warner Home Video (UK), 2003.

The Outsider, Netflix, 2018.

To All the Boys I've Loved Before, Netflix, 2018.

Truong, Kevin. "After 'Sexual Racism' Accusations, Gay Dating App Grindr Gets 'Kindr.'" *NBC News*, September 22, 2018. https://www.nbcnews.com/feature/nbc-out/after-sexual-racism-accusations-gay-day-app-grindr-gets-kindr-n912196.

Truong, Kevin. "Asian American Man Plans Lawsuit to Stop 'Sexual Racism' on Grindr." *NBC News*, July 13, 2018.https://www.nbcnews.com/feature/nbc-out/Asian American-man-threatens-class-action-discrimination-suit-against-grindr-n890946.

US Department of State Office of The Historian. "Repeal of the Chinese Exclusion Act, 1943." Accessed on March 23, 2020.

https://history.state.gov/milestones/1937-1945/chinese-exclu-sion-act-repeal.

US Department of State Office of The Historian. "The Immigration Act of 1924 (The Johnson-Reed Act)." Accessed on March 23, 2020.https://history.state.gov/milestones/1921-1936/immigra-tion-act.

Urban Dictionary. s.v. "Asian Penis." Accessed April 6, 2020. https://www.urbandictionary.com/define.php?term=asian%20penis.

Urban Dictionary. s.v. "Rice Queen." Accessed June 6, 2020. https://www.urbandictionary.com/define.php?term=rice%20queen.

"What Hollywood Movies Do to Perpetuate Racial Stereotypes." *DW News.* Accessed May 13, 2020. https://www.dw.com/en/hollywood-movies-stereotypes-prejudice-data-analy-sis/a-47561660.

Wigodsky, H.S. and R.R. Greene. "The Effect of Testosterone, Estrone, and Estradiol Applied Locally to the Penis of the Rat." *Endocrinology* 26, no. 6, (June 1940): 1078–1080. https://doi.org/10.1210/endo-26-6-1078.

Wilkins, C. L., J. F. Chan, & C. R. Kaiser. "Racial Stereotypes and Interracial Attraction: Phenotypic Prototypicality and Per-ceived Attractiveness of Asians." *Cultural Diversity and Ethnic Minority Psychology* 17, no. 4 (2011): 427–431.

Wilson, Patrick A., Pamela Valera, Ana Ventuneac, Ivan Balan, Matt Rowe, & Alex Carballo-Dieguez. "Race-Based Sexual Stereotyping and Sexual Partnering among Men Who Use the Internet to Identify Other Men for Bareback Sex." *Journal of Sex Research* 46, no. 5 (Fall 2009): 399–413. https://doi.org/10.1080/00224490902846479.

CHAPTER 4

Asian Pacific Institute on Gender-Based Violence. "Culture & Gender-Based Violence." Last modified September 28, 2020. https://www.api-gbv.org/about-gbv/our-analysis/culture-and-gbv/.

Asian Pacific Institute on Gender-Based Violence. "Lifecourse Experiences of Intimate Partner Violence and Help-Seeking among Filipina, India, and Pakistani Women, 2010." Last modified April 22, 2020. https://www.api-gbv.org/resources/lifecourse-ipv-help-seeking/.

Asian Pacific Institute on Gender-Based Violence. "Statistics on Violence against API Women." Last modified October 1, 2020. https://www.api-gbv.org/about-gbv/statistics-violence-against-api-women/.

Bash, Dana, Bridget Nolan, Nelli Black, and Patricia DiCarlo. "Exclusive: Evelyn Yang Reveals She Was Sexually Assaulted by Her OB-GYN While Pregnant." *CNN Politics,* January 17, 2020.

https://www.cnn.com/2020/01/16/politics/evelyn-yang-interview-assault/index.html.

Berdahl, Jennifer L. and Ji-A Min. "Prescriptive Stereotypes and Workplace Consequences for East Asia in North America." *Cultural Diversity and Ethnic Minority Psychology* 18, no. 2 (2012): 141–152. https://doi.org/10.1037/a0027692.

Black, M.C., K.C. Basile, M.J. Breiding, S.G. Smith, J. Chen, K.C. Basile, L.K. Gilbert, M.T. Merrick, N. Patel, M. Walling, and Jain, A, "The National Intimate Partner and Sexual Violence Survey (NISVS): 2010-2012 State Report," *Atlanta, GA: National Center for Injury Prevention and Control, Centers for Disease Control and Prevention,* 2017.

Blackburn, Sarah-SoonLing. "What Is the Model Minority Myth?" *Teaching Tolerance,* March 21, 2019. https://www.tolerance.org/magazine/what-is-the-model-minority-myth.

BrendioEEE. "Why Incels Go after Asian Women." Uploaded on October 28, 2018. YouTube video. https://www.youtube.com/watch?v=h-N8M-Swg3k.

Chang, Doris F., Biing-Jiun Shen, and David Takeuchi. "Prevalence and Demographic Correlates of Intimate Partner Violence in Asian Americans." *International Journal of Law and Psychiatry* 32, no. 3 (2009): 167–175. https://doi.org/10.1016/j.ijlp.2009.02.004.

Cheryan, S., and G. V. Bodenhausen. "Model Minority." In S. M. Caliendo & C. D. McIlwain (Eds), *Routledge Companion to Race & Ethnicity.* New York: Routledge, 2011:173–176.

Chiu, Rowena. "Harvey Weinstein Told Me He Liked Chinese Girls." *The New York Times,* October 5, 2019. https://www.nytimes.com/2019/10/05/opinion/sunday/harvey-weinstein-rowena-chiu.html.

Cho, Sumi K. "Converging Stereotypes in Racialized Sexual Harassment: Where the Model Minority Meets Suzie Wong." *The Journal of Gender, Race, & Justice* 177, no. 1 (1997–1998).

Chow, Kat. "Odds Favor White Men, Asian Women on Dating App." *NPR Code Switch*, November 30, 2013. https://www.npr.org/sections/codeswitch/2013/11/30/247530095/are-you-interested-dating-odds-favor-white-men-asian-women.

Dictionary.com Slang Dictionary. s.v. "incel." Accessed March 18, 2020. https://www.dictionary.com/e/slang/incel/.

Herrema, Martin. "Incels Documentary Featuring Kent Digital Culture Expert Attracts Wide Media Coverage." *University of Kent News Centre,* July 31, 2019. https://www.kent.ac.uk/news/society/23009/incels-documentary-featuring-kent-digital-culture-expert-attracts-wide-media-coverage#:~:-text=Incels%20is%20a%20portmanteau%20of,sexual%20partner%20despite%20desiring%20one.

History.com. "US Immigration Since 1965." Last modified June 7, 2019. https://www.history.com/topics/immigration/us-immigration-since-1965.

Hu, Cathy. "What We Know about Intimate Partner Violence in Asian American and Pacific Islander Communities." *Urban Institute,* May 31, 2018. https://www.urban.org/urban-wire/what-we-know-about-intimate-partner-violence-Asian American-and-pacific-islander-communities.

Kawahara, Debra. "The Bamboo Ceiling: Asian Americans and the Myth of the Model Minority." *Alliant International Univer-*

sity, May 26, 2020. https://www.alliant.edu/blog/bamboo-ceiling-Asian Americans-and-myth-model-minority.

Lim, Audrea. "The Alt-Right's Asian Fetish." *The New York Times,* January 6, 2018. https://www.nytimes.com/2018/01/06/opinion/sunday/alt-right-asian-fetish.html?auth=login-email&login=e-mail.

Ma, Alexandra. "Asian Women Find It Harder Than Ever to Speak Out about Sexual Assault. Evelyn Yang's Story Is Challenging That." *Insider,* January 18, 2020. https://www.insider.com/evelyn-yang-sexual-assault-story-shows-asian-model-minority-pressure-2020-1?fbclid=IwARoJ_LDgQpMIsaLrLUyhNfi-AQj9dH3FkjaD-tfqEwnFy7w8ykmh3tNr1AGw.

Merriam-Webster.com Dictionary. s.v. "Hypergamy." Accessed March 15, 2020. https://www.merriam-webster.com/dictionary/hypergamy.

Merriam-Webster.com Dictionary. s.v. "alt-right." Accessed March 15, 2020. https://www.merriam-webster.com/dictionary/alt-right.

Miller, Chanel. *Know My Name: A Memoir* (New York City: Viking Books, 2020), 250.

"The Model Minority Myth." *The Practice* 5, no. 1 (2018). https://thepractice.law.harvard.edu/article/the-model-minority-myth/.

National Asian Pacific American Women's Forum. "Economic Justice." Accessed May 16, 2020. https://www.napawf.org/economic-justice.

Public Broadcasting Service. "Do Asian Women Have White Fever?" Uploaded May 5, 2013. https://www.pbs.org/independentlens/videos/do-asian-women-have-white-fever/.

Raj, Anita and Jay G. Silverman. "Intimate Partner Violence Amongst South Asian Women in Greater Boston." *Journal of the American Medical Women's Association* 57, no. 2 (Spring 2002):111–114.

Ramakrishnan, Karthick and Sono Shah. "One Out of Every 7 Asian Immigrants Is Undocumented." *AAPI Data*, September 8, 2017. http://aapidata.com/blog/asian-undoc-1in7/.

Reddit. "The Red Pill." Accessed March 15, 2020. https://www.reddit.com/r/TheRedPill/.

Ro, Christine. "The Docility Myth Flattening Asian Women's Careers." *BBC Worklife*, August 16, 2020. https://www.bbc.com/worklife/article/20200807-the-docility-myth-flattening-asian-womens-careers.

Sehnoy, D. P., R. Neranartkomol, M. Ashok, A. Chiang, A. G. Lam, and S. Leng Trieu. "Breaking Down the Silence: A Study Examining Patterns of Sexual Assault and Subsequent Disclosure among Ethnic Groups of Asian Pacific Islander College Women." *Californian Journal of Health Promotion* 7, no. 2 (2009): 78–91.

https://doi.org/10.32398/cjhp.v7i2.2016.

Shah, A. M. *The Structure of Indian Society: Then and Now.* New Delhi: Routledge India, 2012.

Solon, Olivia. "'Incel': Reddit Bans Misogynist Men's Group Blaming Women for Their Celibacy." *The Guardian,* November 8, 2017. https://www.theguardian.com/technology/2017/nov/08/reddit-incel-involuntary-celibate-men-ban.

Stanford Encyclopedia of Philosophy. "Double Consciousness." First published March 21, 2016. https://plato.stanford.edu/entries/double-consciousness/.

Sugarman, David B. and Gerald T. Hotaling. "Intimate Violence and Social Desirability: A Meta–Analytic Review." *Journal of Interpersonal Violence 12, no. 2* (1997): 275–290. https://doi.org/10.1177/088626097012002008.

Sullivan, Andrew. "Why Do Democrats Feel Sorry for Hillary Clinton?" *Intelligencer,* April 14, 2017.

https://nymag.com/intelligencer/2017/04/why-do-democrats-feel-sorry-for-hillary-clinton.html.

Talmazan, Yuliya. "Chanel Miller, Woman Sexually Assaulted by Brock Turner, Speaks Out in First Interview." *NBC News,* September 23, 2019. https://www.nbcnews.com/news/us-news/chanel-miller-woman-sexually-assaulted-brock-turner-speaks-out-first-n1057491.

Thomas, Dexter. "A Lot of White Supremacists Seem to Have an Asian Fetish," *Vice News*, September 12, 2017. https://www.vice.com/en_us/article/d3xwwv/a-lot-of-white-supremacists-seem-to-have-an-asian-fetish.

U.S. Census Bureau. "Statistical Abstract of the United States: 2006." Published November 30, 2005. https://www.census.gov/library/publications/2005/compendia/statab/125ed.html.

Yoshihama, Mieko. "Domestic Violence against Women of Japanese Descent in Los Angeles: Two Methods of Estimating Prevalence." *Violence Against Women* 5 (1999): 869–897. https://doi.org/10.1177/10778019922181536.

CHAPTER 5

AsianLadyOnline.com. "Never Too Late to Fall in Love." Accessed September 2, 2020. https://www.asianladyonline.com/.

Bright Brides. "How to Find the Best Mail Order Bride." Accessed September 2, 2020. https://brightbrides.org.

"Cho Ju-bin: South Korea Chatroom Sex Abuse Suspect Named after Outcry." *BBC News*, March 25, 2020. https://www.bbc.com/news/world-asia-52030219.

Davy, Deanna. "Regional Overview: Sexual Exploitation of Children in Southeast Asia." *ECPAT International*, March 12, 2018.

Diotallevi, Marina ed. *WTO Statement on the Prevention of Organized Sex Tourism*. Cairo (Egypt): World Tourism Organization. Archived from the original on 14 August 2003. Retrieved

24 December 2014. Adopted by the General Assembly of the World Tourism Organization at its eleventh session - Cairo (Egypt), 17–22 October 1995 (Resolution A/RES/338 (XI)).

Dr. Gail Dines: Anti-Porn Scholar, Activist, and Speaker. "About." Accessed August 20, 2020. https://www.gaildines.com/

Enough is Enough. "Sexual Predators/Exploitation/Child Pornography." Last modified September 22, 2020. https://enough.org/stats_exploitation.

Feuerherd, Ben. "Suspect Arrested after Missing Teen Girl Was Spotted on Pornhub." *New York Post*, October 24, 2019. https://nypost.com/2019/10/24/mom-finds-missing-teen-girl-by-spotting-her-on-pornhub/.

"5 Facts You Better Know about Asian Brides." *Foreign Brides*, October 2, 2018. https://foreign-brides.net/blog/facts-about-asian-brides.

Franks, Mary Anne. "Drafting an Effective 'Revenge Porn' Law: A Guide for Legislators." *Cyber Rights Initiative*, September 22, 2016. https://www.cybercivilrights.org/guide-to-legislation/.

Garmoe, Patrick-John. "Rapists Place Losing Bet on Victims' Silence." *The Courier*, June 4, 2011. https://wcfcourier.com/b-rapists-place-losing-bet-on-victims-silence-b/article_b91e2fa3-af57-5b70-8554-f5f1f4325693.html.

Gossett, Jennifer Lynn and Sarah Byrne. "Click Here: A Content Analysis of Internet Rape Sites." *Gender and*

Society 16, no. 5 (October 2002): 689–709. https://doi. org/10.1177/089124302236992.

Hald, Gert Martin, Neil M. Malamuth, and Theis Lange. "Pornography and Sexist Attitudes among Heterosexuals." *Journal of Communication* 63, no. 4 (October 2013): 638–660. https://doi. org/10.1111/jcom.12037.

Hanson, Christopher. "Mail-Order Bride Business Booms in Backlash to US Feminism." *Reuters N. Eur. Service*, Apr. 27, 1987.

"How Big Is Porn?" *Forbes*, May 25, 2001. https://www.forbes. com/2001/05/25/0524porn.html#73b7ed647984.

Hull, Megan. "Pornography Facts and Statistics." The Recovery Village, August 4, 2020.

https://www.therecoveryvillage.com/process-addiction/ porn-addiction/related/pornography-statistics/#gref.

Human Rights Watch. "Owed Justice: Thai Women Trafficked into Debt Bondage in Japan." September, 2000. https://www.hrw. org/reports/2000/japan/.

Internationales Arbeitsamt, Walk Free Foundation, & International Organization for Migration." Global Estimates of Modern Slavery: Forced Labour and Forced Marriage." *International Labour Office*. 2017. https://www.ilo.org/wcmsp5/ groups/public/@dgreports/@dcomm/documents/publication/ wcms_575479.pdf.

Kendall, Todd D. "Pornography, Rape, and the Internet." *The John E. Walker Department of Economics,* 2006.

Kraus, Shane W., Valerie Voon, and Marc N. Potenza. "Should Compulsive Sexual Behavior Be Considered an Addiction?" *Addiction* 111, no. 12 (December 2016): 2097–2106. https://doi.org/10.1111/add.13297.

Kühn, Simone and Jürgen Gallinat. "Brain Structure and Functional Connectivity Associated with Pornography Consumption: The Brain on Porn." *JAMA Psychiatry* 71, no. 7 (July 2014): 827–834. https://doi.org/10.1001/jamapsychiatry.2014.93.

Marsha, Alia. "What's the Deal with Men's Rights Activists and Asian Fetishes?" *Vice News,* January 9, 2018. https://www.vice.com/en_asia/article/9kqqn3/whats-the-deal-with-mens-rights-activists-and-asian-fetishes.

McAndrew, Frank T. "'Mail Order Brides' Still Exist." *Psychology Today,* November 24, 2015. https://www.psychologytoday.com/us/blog/out-the-ooze/201511/mail-order-brides-still-exist.

Meng, Eddy. "Mail-Order Brides: Gilded Prostitution and the Legal Response." *University of Michigan Journal of Law Reform* 28, (1994).

Mohan, Megha. "I Was Raped at 14, and the Video Ended up on a Porn Site." *BBC News,* February 10, 2020. https://www.bbc.com/news/stories-51391981.

O'Briain, Muireann. *Sexual Exploitation of Children and Adolescents in Tourism.* Bangkok: ECPAT International, 2015. https://

www.ecpat.org/wp-content/uploads/2018/02/Regional-Over-view_Southeast-Asia.pdf.

"Officials Arrest 338 Worldwide in Dark Web Child Porn Bust." *Aljazeera*, October 16, 2019. https://www.aljazeera.com/news/2019/10/officials-arrest-338-worldwide-dark-web-child-porn-bust-191016191314375.html?utm_source=website&utm_medium=article_page&utm_campaign=read_more_links.

Oksman, Olga. "Mail-Order Brides: Old Practice Still Seen as New Chance for a Better Life-for Some." *The Guardian*, January 11, 2016. https://www.theguardian.com/lifeandstyle/2016/jan/11/mail-order-marriage-brides-ukraine-america-romance.

Park, Hansol. "South Korea Tackles Hidden Camera Epidemic with Spy Cam Inspection Team." *ABC News*, June 17, 2019. https://abcnews.go.com/International/south-korea-tack-les-hidden-camera-epidemic-spy-cam/story?id=63756405.

Pornhub Insights. "The 2019 Year in Review." Last modified December 11, 2019.https://www.pornhub.com/insights/2019-year-in-review.

Rajratnam, Milind. "Combating Child Pornography in India." *Jurist*, May 14, 2020. https://www.jurist.org/commen-tary/2020/05/milind-rajratnam-combating-child-pornogra-phy/.

Scholes, Robert J. "How Many Mail-Order Brides?" *Immigration Review*, no. 28 (Spring 1997): 7–10.

Shekhar, Shashank. "India Has One of World's Worse Rates of Online Child Pornography Despite Crackdown, Cyber Experts Reveal." *Daily Mail Online,* September 5, 2017. https://www.dailymail.co.uk/indiahome/indianews/article-4855694/India-world-s-worse-rates-online-child-pornography.html.

Shor, Eran and Golshan Golriz. "Gender, Race, and Aggression in Mainstream Pornography." *Archives of Sexual Behavior* 48, no. 3 (April 2019): 739–751. https://doi.org/10.1007/s10508-018-1304-6.

United Nations Human Rights Office of the High Commissioner. "Combating Child Sex Tourism." April 10, 2013.

https://www.ohchr.org/en/newsevents/pages/childsextourism.aspx.

United Nations Office on Drugs and Crime. "Global Report on Trafficking in Persons 2016." *2017.* https://www.unodc.org/documents/data-and-analysis/glotip/2016_Global_Report_on_Trafficking_in_Persons.pdf.

"US Actor Ashton Kutcher Urges End to Child Sexual Exploitation." *BBC News,* February 16, 2017. https://www.bbc.com/news/world-us-canada-38988637.

Watson, Paul. "Mail-Order Bride Firms Flourish in Canada." *TORONTO STAR*, Nov. 9, 1991.

World Health Organization Regional Office for the Western Pacific. "Sex Work in Asia." 2001.

CHAPTER 6

Asian Pacific Policy & Planning Council. "New Data Examines Political Anti-Chinese Rhetoric and Anti-AAPI Hate." Published June 18, 2020. http://www.asianpacificpolicyandplanningcouncil.org/wp-content/uploads/Anti-Chinese_Rhetoric_Press_Release.pdf.

The Bronfenbrenner Center for Translational Research. "How Racism Affects Youth Health and Well-Being." *Psychology Today,* August 27, 2019. https://www.psychologytoday.com/us/blog/evidence-based-living/201908/how-racism-affects-youth-health-and-well-being.

Centers for Disease Control and Prevention. "United States COVID-19 Cases and Deaths by State." Last updated October 10, 2020. https://covid.cdc.gov/covid-data-tracker/?CDC_AA_refVal=https://www.cdc.gov/coronavirus/2019-ncov/cases-updates/cases-in-us.html#cases_casesinlast7days.

Marc, Linda G., Alpa Patel-Larson, H. Irene Hall, Denise Hughes, Margarita Alegría, Georgette Jeanty, Yanick S. Eveillard, Eustache Jean-Louis, and National Haitian American Health Alliance. "HIV among Haitian-Born Persons in the United States, 1985-2007." *AIDS* 24, no. 13 (August, 2010): 2089–2097. https://doi.org/10.1097/QAD.0b013e32833bedff.

Nakamura, David. "With 'Kung Flu,' Trump Sparks Backlash over Racist Language—and a Rallying Cry for Supporters." *The Washington Post,* June 24, 2020. https://www.washingtonpost.com/politics/with-kung-flu-trump-sparks-backlash-over-racist-language--and-a-rallying-cry-for-support-

ers/2020/06/24/485d151e-b620-11ea-aca5-ebb63d27e1ff_story.
html.

Paterson, Jenny, Mark A. Walters, Rupert Brown, and Harriet
Fearn. "Final Report." The Sussex Hate Crime Project, January 2018.

Scherr, Sonia and David Holthouse. "Swine Flu Prompts Anti-Mexican Sentiment." *Southern Poverty Law Center,* August 30,
2009. https://www.splcenter.org/fighting-hate/intelligence-report/2009/swine-flu-prompts-anti-mexican-sentiment.

Stevens, Matt. "How Asian American Leaders Are Grappling with
Xenophobia Amid Coronavirus." *The New York Times,* last
modified April 10, 2020. https://www.nytimes.com/2020/03/29/
us/politics/coronavirus-Asian Americans.html.

Suleman, Shazeen, Kent D. Garber, and Lainie Rutkow. "Xenophobia as a Determinant of Health: An Integrative Review." *Journal of Public Health Policy* 39, no. 9 (September, 2018). https://
doi.org/10.1057/s41271-018-0140-1.

"What Is Yellow Fever?" WebMD. Reviewed on November 2, 2019.
https://www.webmd.com/a-to-z-guides/qa/what-is-yellow-fever.

ACKNOWLEDGMENTS

INDIVIDUALS

ABIGAIL DESCHENES

ADINA STEFAN

ALEXANDRA CHANG

ALLEN KIM

AMANDA KONG

AMANDA LE

AMBER HECKERT

AN DOAN

ANDREW YAN

ANGELA LIU

ANGIE CHEN

ANNIE TSUI

ANTHONY KIM

ARLENE YANG

ASHLEY KYELEM

AZELIA LAU

BRADEN CRONIN

BRANDON KO

BRIAN LIN

CAITLYN LIU

CALEB LI

CANDACE PANG

CANDACE TODD

CAROLINE COCHRAN

CAROLYN ZHANG

CASEY RYU

CATHERINE PARNELL

CHANYOUNG LEE

CHARLOTTE WONG

CHRISTINE KIM

CLAIRE CAI

CYRIN ANNE GELUZCYRIN

DANIEL ANDERSON

DANIEL KONG

DANNY LEE

DASOL LIM

EILEENE LEE

ELICE SHIN

ELIZABETH YOON

ELLE COVER

EMILY KWON

ERIC CHENG

ERIC KOESTER

ESTHER STEVENSON

EUGENE CHOE

EVAN TANG

EYY2991

FATIMA BAXTER

FIONA TEO

FLEMMING LI

FRANCESCA WAI

FREDDIE LIU

GABRIELLE SUN HEE KIM

GENE KIM

GIOVANNI GAMALONG

GLO HARN CHOI

HANNAH FUCHS

HAPPINESS YI

HEEJUN PARK

ISABELL LIU

JACE CHEN

JACOB NAM

JACOB WU

JAEYOUNG YU

JAMIE B

JAMIE LEE

JANICE KHANG

JASON JC LOU

JASON LIU

JASON NGUYEN

JASON XU

JENNA WANG

JENNIFER LEE

JENNY PARK

JEREMIAH KIM

JESS OH

JIHYUN PARK

JIIN RHEW

JOANNE LEE

JOEY PARK

JOHN LEE

JOHN TAN

JORDINA BUHAY

JOSHUA LEE

JOY HSU

JOY KIM

JULIA URIM HWANG

JULIE XU

JUSTIN JI

KAITLYN CHOE

KAITLYN KWON

KAYOUNG KIM

KEREN PARK

KIANA STAPLES

KIERSTEN YOON

LAUREN LEE

LAURYN MADISE

LEWIS ZHUO

LORI ERICKSON

LUCAS NGUYEN

MARVIN FUNG

MARY YANG

MATHEW CHONG
MATTHEW KIM
MICHAEL CHOI
MICHAEL LASFETTO
MICHELLE WONG
MSCAFFEINE
PAUL KIM
RACHEL CHIU
RACHEL KIM
RAGAN FUNKHOUSER
RAY YU
RICHARD LEONG
ROSEMARY DONG
RYAN LEE
RYAN LO
SAMUEL LEE
SANDRA LY
SARAH BARZAK
SARANG PARK
SEONG KIM
SERIN OH
SHARON KANG

SHARON LEE
SHARON WU
SHERRY DU
SHIKARA RINGDAHL
SHIN YOUNG GRACE YU
SOHAE YANG
SOPHIA
SLAWSON-VILLASMIL
SUHAN PARK
SUN JUN
SUNNYHO66
SYDNEY GIL
SYDNEY JI
SYDNEY SIMMONS
TIGRESS74
TRACY ZHANG
TSATSKA ENKHBAYAR
VANESSA TO
XIYUAN WU
YIFAN LEI
YONG BIN CHO
YUFAN YANG

ORGANIZATIONS

42ND PARALLEL
AAPI NARRATIVE
ASIAN ADVOCATES
Asian American CIVIC
SCHOLARS
ASIAN WOMEN COLLEGE
SURVIVORS

ASIAN YOUTH FOR
CIVIC ENGAGEMENT
(AYCE VOTE)
ASIANANDLGBTQ
ASIANS IN THE ARTS
ASIANS LEAD
ASIANS4 ANTIRACISM
CREATIVELY ASIAN

DEAR ASIAN YOUTH
DETESTER MAGAZINE
FRESH OFF THE BROKE
MESSENGER PIGEON
NOT SO MELLOW YELLOW
PODCAST
NSMY CAST
PROJECT VOICE POD
SO YOU WANT TO
TALK ABOUT…
THE UNO SOCIETY
THE YAPPIE
UNCONVENTIONAL
ASIANS
UNMASK THE RACISM
YOUR CHANGE PROVIDER

Made in the USA
Monee, IL
30 March 2021

64276848R00134